# Advent

# A Family Celebration

## Prayers & Activities
## for Each Day

Julie Walters

the**WORD**
among us®

The Word Among Us Press
9639 Dr. Perry Road
Ijamsville, Maryland 21754
www.wordamongus.org

10 09 08 07 06 05 04    1 2 3 4 5 6 7 8

ISBN: 1-59325-041-X

Cover and book design: David Crosson

Made and printed in the United States of America

Library of Congress Catalog Control Number: 2004107598

Cover Art Illustration by Joe Kovach

For my grown children: Christine, Theresa, Monica, and Peter, and their spouses, who show their children and others the face of Christ.

—Julie Walters

# Table of Contents

**Acknowledgments** / 6

**Introduction** / 7

1. **The Blessing of the Advent Wreath** / 9

2. **Reflections for Sundays** / 13
> First Sunday of Advent / 14
> Second Sunday of Advent / 20
> Third Sunday of Advent / 26
> Fourth Sunday of Advent / 32

3. **Reflections for Weekdays** / 39
> First Week of Advent / 40
> Second Week of Advent / 52
> Third Week of Advent / 64
> Fourth Week of Advent / 74

4. **Reflections for Feast Days** / 89

5. **The Jesse Tree** / 95

6. **Advent Angels and the Christ Child Crib** / 121
> **The Little Juggler**

**About the Author** / 127

# Acknowledgments

I am grateful to the many families who shared their Advent celebrations with me and to those who shared how God has worked in their lives. Their stories show that indeed God is working in and through his people today.

I am also grateful to Jill Boughton, who generously allowed me to expand on her family's Advent Litany. I am indebted to Patty Mitchell, my editor, who asked me to write this book. It has been a joy and a rich experience.

Last but not least of all, I'm thankful for my dear friend and husband, Clem, who has cheered me on these past few months.

Special thanks to those who gave of their time to review the manuscript.

# Introduction

Advent is a wonderful time of the year. It's a time of baking, gift making, buying, and wrapping. It's a time of expectant waiting, anticipating, and spiritually preparing for the coming of Christ Jesus.

In the *Office of Readings* for Wednesday of the first week of Advent, a meditation by St. Bernard of Clairvaux reflects on the three comings of Jesus. The first coming is when Jesus was born and lived on earth. The second is when he comes to live in each of us in spirit and power. The third is when he comes again in majesty and glory. *Advent: A Family Celebration* offers prayerful, helpful, and fun ways to live out the four weeks of this beautiful season and to celebrate all three of Jesus' comings.

The major portion of this book is designed to help families reflect each day on the Advent Mass readings. These reflections can be read in conjunction with the lighting of the Advent wreath—a familiar and beloved symbol of Advent used in many Catholic homes. The Advent wreath, with its four candles, helps us to celebrate Christ, the Light who is coming into the world. It also heightens our expectancy of Christ's coming in the flesh, as each week is marked by the lighting of another candle. The daily Scripture readings and reflections reveal the awesome truth that Christ lives in us by the power of the Holy Spirit. We reflect on Christ's working in other situations and become more aware of ways he can work in us and through us to hasten the kingdom of God.

Unless otherwise noted, each day's reflections are based on true stories. Let your children know that these events really happened. They will help your child move from ideas and thoughts about God to recognizing the difference that faith makes in everyday circumstances and decisions. Reflections are offered both for younger children and older children, and are geared to their development and experience. Parents can judge for themselves which ones are appropriate for their families.

Another section of the book provides the framework for parents to make and use a "Jesse Tree." Jesus is "the root of Jesse" (Isaiah 11:1)—he was from the house of King David, and Jesse was David's father. A Jesse Tree traces the history of our redemption from creation through the birth of Jesus. This section features a brief synopsis of a Bible story along with a litany that can be recited each day and suggestions for symbols that can be made or purchased—such as an apple for Adam and Eve or an ark for Noah—to place on the tree. For children, the stories and symbols of the Jesse Tree provide an overview of salvation history and all those Old and New Testament figures who waited patiently for a Savior.

Several additional Advent activities for families are included in this book. Family members can choose to be "Advent angels" to one another and then place a straw in the Christ Child's crib when they perform an "undercover" act of kindness for that person. In addition to being fun, this activity helps us to become more Christlike and builds the kingdom of God in our homes. If our zeal slips a bit, the story of the Little Juggler will cheer us on to serve with love.

Our celebration of Advent prepares us to eagerly welcome Christ at Christmas and when he comes again in glory. Perhaps your children will enjoy this celebration so much that they will echo the sentiments of other children who say: "Oh no! Is Advent over already?"

Julie Walters

# 1

# The Blessing of the Advent Wreath

The Scripture verses in *Advent: A Family Celebration* are taken from the daily Mass readings for each day of Advent. According to the Church's liturgical calendar, the weekday Advent readings are always the same, no matter what the year. But there are three Sunday cycles (A, B, and C), with corresponding readings for each cycle. To determine which Sunday cycle to use, see the chart on the opposite page.

On the first Sunday of Advent, say one of the blessings suggested here and light the first candle of your Advent wreath. Then begin the readings designated for the first Sunday of Advent. On the following day, Monday, begin with the weekday readings for the first week of Advent. The next Sunday, read the reflections for the second week of Advent, and the next day, go to the weekday readings for the second week of Advent.

Proceed in the same manner until you reach the second part of Advent, which begins on December 17. At that point until Christmas Day, follow the calendar dates rather than the days of the week to find the appropriate Mass reading and reflection. (These are included in the reflections for the fourth week of Advent.)

Be on the lookout for the special feast days that fall in Advent: the Feast of St. Andrew (November 30); the Feast of the Immaculate Conception (December 8); and the Feast of Our Lady of Guadalupe (December 12). When your family prays on these days, skip the weekday reading and go instead to Chapter 4, which has readings for that feast day. The next day, return to the regular weekday reading for that day of the week.

Here are the Sunday cycles to use based on the calendar year:

Advent 2004 –Year A
Advent 2005 – Year B
Advent 2006 – Year C
Advent 2007 – Year A
Advent 2008 – Year B
Advent 2009 – Year C

# The Blessing of the Advent Wreath

(To be said on the First Sunday of Advent, when the Advent wreath is assembled and the first candle is lit.)

**Father or Mother:** "Our help is from the Lord our God."

**All:** "Who created all things."

**Father or Mother:** "Father, by your word all things are made holy. Pour out your blessing upon this wreath. Its circle reminds us that you are without beginning or end. You always were and always will be. Its boughs, which are always green, remind us that your love for us never changes. The candlelight reminds us of Jesus, your Son, Light of the World. Grant that we who use this wreath may joyfully prepare our hearts for the coming of Christ Jesus."

**All:** "Amen."

Another Advent blessing that can be used is taken from the *Book of Blessings*, the official prayer book of the American bishops:

**Father or Mother:** "Lord our God, we praise you for your Son, Jesus Christ: he is Emmanuel, the hope of the peoples, he is the wisdom that teaches and guides us, he is the Savior of every nation.

"Lord God, let your blessing come upon us as we light the candles of this wreath. May the wreath and its light be a sign of Christ's promise to bring us salvation. May he come quickly and not delay. We ask this through Christ our Lord."

**All:** "Amen."

# 2

## Reflections for Sundays

# Prayers for the First Week of Advent

Light one purple candle this week.

**Opening prayer:** All make the sign of the cross and say: "May we keep the Lord's words in our hearts and minds."

**Closing prayer:** "Father, open our eyes and hearts to ways we can love while we wait for Jesus."

**Response:** "Let's love while we wait for Jesus."

Or

**Sing:**    O come, O come Emmanuel,
And ransom captive Israel,
That mourns in lonely exile here,
Until the Son of God appear.
Rejoice! Rejoice! Emmanuel
Shall come to thee, O Israel.

End with an "Our Father."

# First Sunday of Advent
## Year A
ISAIAH 2:1-5    PSALM 122:1-9
ROMANS 13:11-14    MATTHEW 24:37-44

**Reading for older children:** "Two will be in the field; one will be taken and one will be left. Two women will be grinding meal together; one will be taken and one will be left. Keep awake therefore, for you do not know on what day your Lord is coming. But understand this: if the owner of the house had known in what part of the night the thief was coming, he would have stayed awake and would not have let his house be broken into. Therefore you also must be ready, for the Son of Man is coming at an unexpected hour." (Matthew 24:40-44)

**Reflection for older children:** This story can make us feel a little fearful. However, Jesus never told stories to make people afraid. He loves us and wants us to be prepared for his coming.

How can we be prepared? Here is a story about one man who was ready. This man tried to live in a way that was pleasing to the Lord. He was a loving and responsible husband and father, and he was generous with his time and money. Then one day, when he was only fifty-two, he suddenly and unexpectedly had a heart attack and died. His wife, his five teenage children, and his friends were shocked.

On the same day that he died, his wife was looking for some important papers in the family safe. There she found letters her husband had written to his children. The letters, which expressed the father's love, hopes, and wishes for each of his children, were a great comfort to all of them. The father did not know the time Christ would come for him, but he was prepared.

Are you prepared for Jesus' coming? What would you do differently today if you knew that Jesus was coming tomorrow?

**Reading for younger children:** Many peoples shall come and say, "Come, let us go up to the mountain of the LORD, to the house of the God of Jacob; that he may teach us his ways and that we may walk in his paths." (Isaiah 2:3)

**Reflection for younger children:** How does God want us to walk in his path? God's ways are loving, and that's the path he wants us to walk.

Amy's feelings were hurt. She had always been friendly with Michele, a classmate, but lately Michele had stopped talking to her. Amy didn't know why, so she asked Michele if she was angry with her. Michele said no, but she still refused to play with Amy at recess or sit next to her at the lunch table.

Amy talked to her mom about the problem. Her mom said, "You can't control what Michele does, but you can control what you do. Be friendly to Michele even if she is unfriendly to you. And even if you are upset with her, don't talk about her behind her back."

Amy tried to take her mother's advice. Over the next few weeks, Michele started to warm up. Soon Michele was talking to her again and acting friendly. Amy was glad she had been kind to Michele, even when Michele hadn't been friendly to her.

Think of someone in your life with whom you could be more loving. Decide today to show your love and to walk in God's ways.

# First Sunday of Advent
## Year B

ISAIAH 63:16-17, 19; 64:2-7   PSALM 80:2-3, 15-16, 18-19
1 CORINTHIANS 1:3-9   MARK 13:33-37

**Reading for older children:** You, O LORD, are our father; our Redeemer from of old is your name. (Isaiah 63:16)

**Reflection for older children:** The prophet Isaiah was beseeching God to rescue the Israelites from their enemies. He recalled all the great things that God had done for his people in the past. Then he appealed to God by pointing out that God was the Father of his people. A father will not turn his back on his children.

When we are suffering, we may be tempted to think that God has turned his back on us. But the same truth applies to us: God is our Father. By our baptism, we have become his children. We can go to him with our troubles, and he will listen. He loves us even more than our earthly fathers.

The next time you are tempted to doubt God's care for you, remember this Scripture verse and say, "You, Lord, are my Father!"

**Reading for younger children:** "But about that day or hour no one knows, neither the angels in heaven, nor the Son, but only the Father. Beware, keep alert; for you do not know when the time will come." (Mark 13:32-33)

**Reflection for younger children:** In Mark's Gospel, Jesus tells us that God the Father alone knows when he—Jesus—will come again. That's why Jesus encourages us to be alert. "Alert" means that we are awake and watchful. How can we practice being alert? One way is to be alert to the needs of others.

Claire, a child of seven with Down's Syndrome, was alert to the needs of her grandmother. Claire's grandmother had Alzheimer's disease. One morning her grandmother was very confused. She didn't know where she was or who Claire's mother and her grandchildren were. Then Claire took her grandmother's hand and led her to a wall where photographs of the family hung.

She said, "Grandma, let me introduce you to your family." As Claire pointed to each photo, she said the person's name. Soon her grandmother was peaceful.

## First Sunday of Advent
## Year C

JEREMIAH 33:14-16  PSALM 25:4-5, 8-10, 14
1 THESSALONIANS 3:12—4:2  LUKE 21:25-28, 34-36

**Reading for older children:** Lead me in your truth, and teach me, for you are the God of my salvation; for you I wait all day long. (Psalm 25:5)

**Reflection for older children:** As a young man, St. Augustine searched for truth. Augustine lived in northern Africa in the second half of the fourth century. When he was eighteen, he became a Manichee. Manichees considered themselves Christians, but they had many unchristian beliefs. Augustine's mother, St. Monica, prayed fervently for her son to find the truth of Christianity.

When he was twenty-nine, Augustine moved to Milan and was intrigued by the preaching of the bishop there, St. Ambrose. However, Augustine remained in despair of ever discovering the truth. As he continued his search, he read many books and realized that many of his former ideas were flawed. One day he knew he had to make a decision to leave behind the sin in his life and to become a Christian. He heard a voice urging him to "pick up and read," so he picked up the Bible and opened to a verse that told him to "put on the Lord Jesus Christ" (Romans 13:14). Peace immediately flooded his heart. Augustine had found the truth of Christ! He spent the remainder of his life serving God—as a bishop and a tireless defender of the Catholic faith.

**Reading for younger children:** And may the Lord make you increase and abound in love for one another and for all, just as we abound in love for you. (1 Thessalonians 3:12)

**Reflection for younger children:** To abound in love means that love overflows as good deeds. Doing good increases our love, so we become more like Jesus.

One fall day, six fifth-grade boys were like Christ to an elderly couple. They gathered to play football when one of the boys told his friend whose yard they were using, "Wow! Look at all those leaves in your neighbor's yard."

"Yeah! Usually Mr. Nelson's yard is the cleanest, but he hurt his back last week," said the neighbor boy.

"Well, let's rake his yard for him," one of the other boys suggested.

As the boys raked, they saw Mr. and Mrs. Nelson at the window with tears in their eyes. Mr. Nelson offered to pay the boys, but they declined. Their payment was the happiness that comes from loving others.

# Prayers for the Second Week of Advent

Light two purple candles this week.

**Opening prayer:** All make the sign of the cross and say: "May we keep the Lord's words in our hearts and minds."

**Closing prayer:** "Father, give us strength for doing good, so we can prepare the way for Jesus."

**Response:** "Jesus is coming! Prepare the way for the Lord!"

Or

**Sing:**    O Come, thou wisdom from on high,
Who orders all things mightily,
To us the path of knowledge show,
And teach us in her ways to go.
Rejoice! Rejoice! Emmanuel
Shall come to thee, O Israel.

End with an "Our Father."

# Second Sunday of Advent
## Year A
ISAIAH 11:1-10  PSALM 72:1-2, 7-8, 12-13, 17
ROMANS 15:4-9  MATTHEW 3:1-12

**Reading for older children:** Welcome one another, therefore, just as Christ has welcomed you, for the glory of God. (Romans 15:7)

**Reflection for older children:** Each day we can find opportunities to be Christ to those we don't know. We can be as welcoming as Jesus would be to us. Have you ever heard this anecdote about a high school student who unknowingly made a huge difference in someone's life because he was welcoming?

When Jake was a high school freshman, he spotted a new kid coming out of school carrying a huge pile of books. Jake thought, "What a nerd!" Then a group of boys came along and knocked the books out of the boy's arms and threw him in the dirt. Jake saw a terrible sadness in the boy's eyes as he ran over to help him pick up his books. The boy, whose name was Frank, lived near Jake, so he carried some of his books to his house. Then Jake invited him to play football with some of his friends. They hung around together that weekend, and over the next four years they became good friends. Frank became a popular boy and class valedictorian.

After graduation, Frank told Jake that the day he helped pick up his books, he had cleaned out his locker because he planned to commit suicide. It was Jake's welcoming friendship that saved him.

**Reading for younger children:** This is the one of whom the prophet Isaiah spoke when he said, "The voice of one crying out in the wilderness: 'Prepare the way of the Lord, make his paths straight.' " (Matthew 3:3)

**Reflection for younger children:** John the Baptist loved God and wanted to do his will. God asked John to prepare a path for Jesus by preaching about the forgiveness of sins. Here's a story about a grandfather with Alzheimer's disease who, out of love for his daughter and her family, prepared a "safe path" for them.

The grandfather was often very confused. There were times when he didn't recognize his family and didn't know where he was. But whenever a prayer was said, he bowed his head and folded his hands.

One cold winter morning, his daughter needed to take her baby to the doctor. First she carefully helped the other children down the icy steps and into the van. Her father had followed her, and waited at the bottom of the steps while she went into the house for the baby. When she started down the steps, she saw that her father had taken a sharp stick and chipped away the ice on the steps. His love had prepared the way.

# Second Sunday of Advent
## Year B
ISAIAH 40:1-5, 9-11   PSALM 85:9-14
2 PETER 3:8-14   MARK 1:1-8

**Reading for older children:** Comfort, O comfort my people, says your God. Speak tenderly to Jerusalem, and cry to her that she has served her term, that her penalty is paid, that she has received from the LORD's hand double for all her sins. (Isaiah 40:1-2)

**Reflection for older children:** In London's National Gallery, a painting by Filippino Lippi called *The Virgin and Child with St. John* depicts baby Jesus on Mary's lap holding a red pomegranate, a symbol of the Passion. St. John, a small boy holding a golden cross, gazes up at Jesus.

The painting reminds us of the truth that Jesus was born to die, to redeem us, to pay for our sins by his blood on the cross. It's as if you and I were going to jail for stealing a million dollars, but Jesus paid the million to the person from whom we stole it. Then Jesus set us free and gave us two million dollars! But Jesus has given us more than money. He has given us forgiveness of our sins and eternal life.

**Reading for younger children:** "See, I am sending my messenger ahead of you, who will prepare your way; the voice of one crying out in the wilderness: 'Prepare the way of the Lord, make his paths straight.' " (Mark 1:2-3)

**Reflection for younger children:** Prayer is one way to "prepare the way of the Lord." During a civil war in Lebanon in 1982, Blessed Mother Teresa of Calcutta tried to convince officials to allow her into West Beirut to rescue Muslim children who were trapped in a hospital that had been bombed. Officials told her that she could not cross the line from East to West Beirut until the fighting was over.

Mother Teresa insisted that there would be a ceasefire the next day. She told them she had prayed to the Blessed Virgin Mary for a ceasefire on the day before her feast day, the Feast of the Assumption, on August 15.

The following day, there was a ceasefire. It lasted long enough for the Red Cross to take Mother Teresa and several of her sisters to the shelter. They rescued thirty-seven frightened and starving children. Mother Teresa's prayer had been heard.

## Second Sunday of Advent
### Year C
BARUCH 5:1-9   PSALM 126:1-6
PHILIPPIANS 1:4-6, 8-11   LUKE 3:1-6

**Reading for older children:** And this is my prayer, that your love may overflow more and more with knowledge and full insight to help you to determine what is best, so that in the day of Christ you may be pure and blameless, having produced the harvest of righteousness that comes through Jesus Christ for the glory and praise of God. (Philippians 1:9-11)

**Reflection for older children:** In order to be pure and blameless as St. Paul urges, we must intelligently weigh what is the best thing to say and do.

When a high school student ignored a friend in the school hallway, she felt regretful afterward and wondered why she had acted so rudely. In thinking about it, she realized her rudeness was the result of a negative conversation she had had with another girl about her friend.

There is a direct connection between our thoughts, words, and actions. Conversations, movies, music, books, TV programs, video games: All influence our thought patterns. Whenever we realize a train of thought is negative or leading us toward sin, we must stop it and replace it with a good thought. Allowing only righteous thoughts into our minds will result in good actions and give glory and praise to God.

**Reading for younger children:** [John the Baptist] went into all the region around the Jordan, proclaiming a baptism of repentance for the forgiveness of sins. (Luke 3:3)

**Reflection for younger children:** John the Baptist told people to prepare for Jesus by being sorry for their sins and asking for forgiveness. One way we can prepare for Jesus' coming is to forgive those who have wronged us.

Mandy always walked home from school with two sisters who lived next door. One day the sisters didn't wait for her, and she walked home alone. Later they told Mandy that their older brother didn't like her and forced them to leave without her.

Mandy was angry and hurt. She cried when she told her mother about the incident. Her mother said, "Mandy, you can forgive his meanness even if he doesn't say he is sorry. You know how it feels when you ask forgiveness and are forgiven. It's as if a big weight is lifted off your shoulders. It's the same when you forgive. You just have to say the words, 'I will forgive him.' "

Mandy did forgive the neighbor boy. And after awhile, the anger and hurt left her.

# Prayers for the Third Week of Advent

Light two purple candles and one pink or white candle this week.

**Daily opening prayer:** All make the sign of the cross and say: "May we keep the Lord's words in our hearts and minds."

**Closing prayer:** "Father, give us new zeal to love others. Let us rejoice as we eagerly await the coming of Jesus."

**Response:** "Rejoice! Jesus is coming soon! Let us love with new zeal as we eagerly wait for him."

Or

**Sing:**    O come, O come, thou Lord of Might,
Who to the tribes on Sinai's height
In ancient times did give the law,
In power, majesty and awe.
Rejoice! Rejoice! Emmanuel
Shall come to thee, O Israel.

End with an "Our Father."

# Third Sunday of Advent
## Year A

Isaiah 35:1-6, 10  Psalm 146:6-10
James 5:7-10  Matthew 11:2-11

**Reading for older children:** Jesus answered them, "Go and tell John what you hear and see: the blind receive their sight, the lame walk, the lepers are cleansed, the deaf hear, the dead are raised, and the poor have good news brought to them." (Matthew 11:4-5)

**Reflection for older children:** The good news is not just for people who lived in Jesus' time. It's for us today as well. Here's how two college graduates brought the good news of God's kingdom to the poor.

After graduation, they decided to move to a poor, inner-city neighborhood. Some of their friends joined them. Some stayed two or three weeks, others for a month, and others for a year or two. In two years, they had built three new houses, repaired other houses in the neighborhood, visited the neighbors, ate and prayed with them, and taught their children at a summer camp.

These two young men could have decided to live in more comfortable circumstances. But they wanted to share their lives with those in need. As they lived among their neighbors, they brought them the good news that God loves them.

**Reading for younger children:** The LORD lifts up those who are bowed down; the LORD loves the righteous. (Psalm 146:8)

**Reflection for younger children:** Have you ever felt sad, and then someone "lifted" your spirits and made you feel happy again? Here's a story about a girl named Laura, who "lifted up" her younger cousin and helped her to do the right thing.

Laura was excited. Today was the day for swimming, tubing, and water skiing at a nearby lake. Everyone in her family was going— parents, grandparents, aunts, uncles, and cousins—and they were all busy getting ready to leave. Then a hush descended over the confusion. One of the cousins was crying in her father's arms. She had promised her soccer coach that she would play that day so that her team would not have to forfeit the game. But she really wanted to go to the lake with everyone else.

Laura said, "Would you like me to go to the game with you? It only takes an hour. I'd like to do that, if you want me to." The little cousin hugged Laura tightly. "Would you?" she asked. Laura's kindness helped her cousin to support her team and to go to her game with a smile on her face.

## Third Sunday of Advent
### Year B
ISAIAH 61:1-2, 10-11   (PSALM) LUKE 1:46-50, 53-54
1 THESSALONIANS 5:16-24   JOHN 1:6-8, 19-28

**Reading for older children:** The spirit of the Lord GOD is upon me, because the Lord has anointed me; he has sent me to bring good news to the oppressed, to bind up the brokenhearted. (Isaiah 61:1)

**Reflection for older children:** How can we "bring good news to the oppressed" or "bind up the brokenhearted" this Advent?

Here's what one group of friends did to bind up the brokenhearted.

Several families in the city had experienced heartbreaking losses during the past year. In the summer, a seven-year-old girl had died in a traffic accident. In the fall, a single mother's sixteen-year-old son had taken his own life. The young father of another family had died unexpectedly. A daughter from another family had been shot to death.

The "Christmas Commandoes," as members of the group called themselves, remembered these families at Christmastime. They secretly decorated their front yards and left gifts on their steps. They also left notes explaining that they knew Christmas this year would be difficult. They shared in their sorrow and enormous loss, and hoped the gifts would bring joy, because they were given in the spirit of love.

**Reading for younger children:** Rejoice always, pray without ceasing, give thanks in all circumstances; for this is the will of God in Christ Jesus for you. (1 Thessalonians 5:16-18)

**Reflection for younger children:** God wants us to thank him for all that he gives us, but he is also pleased when we thank one another. How often do we remember to thank our moms, dads, brothers, sisters, or other family members?

One family's birthday traditions include giving thanks for the person whose birthday is being celebrated. After the dinner, parents, brothers, sisters, and any other relatives who are present tell the guest of honor how he or she has been a blessing to them over the past year. One year, a seven-year-old girl told her eight-year-old cousin, "I'm thankful you always include me when we play."

Even if no one in your family is celebrating a birthday today, think of one thing you can thank a family member for.

# Third Sunday of Advent
## Year C
### Zephaniah 3:14-18 (Psalm) Isaiah 12:2-6
### Philippians 4:4-7 Luke 3:10-18

**Reading for older children:** Sing aloud, O daughter Zion; shout, O Israel! Rejoice and exult with all your heart, O daughter Jerusalem! . . . I will remove disaster from you. (Zephaniah 3:14, 18)

**Reflection for older children:** The Lord saved Janet, the school district's head dietician, and another food service employee from near disaster. They went to check a new walk-in refrigerator that was housed in an unused school. They walked into the refrigerator, and as the door closed, they noticed there were no safety bars on the inside of the door. They were locked inside, and the temperature was below zero.

They began to yell and pound on the door, even though they had seen no one in the building or any cars in the lot. After yelling for about twenty minutes, Janet said, "We're in a very dangerous situation. I think we'd better pray that someone finds us."

No sooner had they started praying than a maintenance man opened the door. He explained that as he was driving by the school, he remembered that he needed to replace a light bulb inside the refrigerator.

God had "removed disaster" from these two women when the Holy Spirit prompted this man to remember the burned-out light bulb. And because the man listened, he ended up saving two lives!

**Reading for younger children:** Rejoice in the Lord always; again I will say, Rejoice. . . . Do not worry about anything, but in everything by prayer and supplication with thanksgiving let your requests be made known to God. (Philippians 4:46)

**Reflection for younger children:** These words from the Bible tell us not to worry. It's easy to fall into the habit of worrying. St. Paul tells us in this Scripture verse that instead of worrying, we should ask God to help us.

Every night before he had a test, Michael would start to worry. Even though he studied hard, he still worried that he wouldn't know the answers and would fail. One evening before a big test, while his dad was quizzing him, he noticed how worried Michael was. He suggested they pray together. They prayed that Michael would stop worrying and would do well on the test.

The next day, every time Michael was tempted to worry about the test, he would say a prayer to God, asking for help to stop his worrying. When the time came to take the test, instead of the usual butterflies in his stomach, Michael felt calm. Even though there were a few questions he wasn't sure about, he stayed calm throughout the test and didn't even think about it when it was over. Michael decided that he would pray every time he had a test. God would help him to break his worry habit and to trust in him!

# Prayers for the Fourth Week of Advent

Light all four candles this week.

**Opening prayer:** All make the sign of the cross and say: "May we keep the Lord's words in our hearts and minds."

**Closing prayer:** "Our Christ is near. Let him find us loving one another when he comes."

**Response:** "Come, Lord Jesus, come quickly!"

Or

**Sing:**  O come, thou Rod of Jesse's stem,
From every foe deliver them
That trust thy mighty power to save,
And give them vic'try o'er the grave.
Rejoice! Rejoice! Emmanuel
Shall come to thee, O Israel.

End with an "Our Father."

# Fourth Sunday of Advent
## Year A
ISAIAH 7:10-14  PSALM 24:1-6
ROMANS 1:1-7  MATTHEW 1:18-24

**Reading for older children:** [Jesus], who was descended from David according to the flesh . . . was declared to be Son of God with power according to the spirit of holiness by resurrection from the dead. (Romans 1:3-4)

**Reflection for older children:** Jesus came into the world to give us eternal life. Scripture promises that on the day of final judgment, if we have followed the Lord, we will be resurrected from the dead, just like Jesus was on Easter. Our souls will be reunited with "glorified" bodies that will never age or decay.

The *Catechism of the Catholic Church* notes that "how" this will happen "exceeds our imagination and understanding," and can be understood only through faith (CCC, 1000). We do know that it is only through the power of Jesus' resurrection that we will also be resurrected on the last day. That is why we are so grateful to Jesus for his coming at Christmas. He came into the world so that he could conquer death for us, for all time.

**Reading for younger children:** Her husband Joseph, being a righteous man and unwilling to expose her to public disgrace, planned to dismiss her quietly. But just when he had resolved to do this, an angel of the Lord appeared to him in a dream and said, "Joseph, son of David, do not be afraid to take Mary as your wife, for the child conceived in her is from the Holy Spirit." (Matthew 1:19-20)

**Reflection for younger children:** Angels appear for many different reasons. The angel Gabriel appeared to Joseph to assure him it was God's plan to take Mary as his wife. Sometimes the Lord sends angels to comfort us.

An angel once appeared to a little boy in the hospital to bring him comfort and peace. He was being treated for cancer, and he was feeling lonely and afraid. One night he called a nurse into his room and asked her, "Who was the shiny bright lady standing at the end of my bed?" The nurse had been at her station outside his room, and no one had gone in or out of his room. "God must have sent you an angel to help you get better," she told the little boy. He smiled and fell peacefully to sleep.

## Fourth Sunday of Advent
### Year B
2 Samuel 7:1-5, 8-12, 14, 16   Psalm 89:2-5, 27, 29
Romans 16:25-27   Luke 1:26-38

**Reading for older children:** Now to God who is able to strengthen you according to my gospel and the proclamation of Jesus Christ . . . to whom be the glory forever! Amen. (Romans 16:25, 27)

**Reflection for older children:** God is our strength, and he can strengthen us when we call upon him. Our Father has strengthened Laurie and Dick, and they draw others to Christ through their lives of faithfulness and joy.

Twenty-seven years ago, as they were making final wedding plans, Laurie, a nurse, began dropping instruments in surgery. At first she thought it was wedding jitters, but when other strange symptoms appeared, she consulted a doctor. Tests revealed she had multiple sclerosis, an incurable disease.

Laurie pleaded with Dick to release her from their marriage commitment. But Dick refused, saying that whatever the future held, they would face it together with Christ. And they did face it—praying, laughing, and crying together.

Over the years, Laurie's condition gradually worsened until Dick could no longer care for her at home. He found a well-staffed, pleasant nursing home where he visits her daily. Laurie accompanies Dick to office parties in her wheelchair, showing off her fingernails, Dick's "paint job." She can't speak very well anymore, but she loves to listen to stories, and her smile and laughter are contagious. Laurie and Dick face each day with the strength of the Lord.

**Reading for younger children:** The angel said to [Mary], "The Holy Spirit will come upon you, and the power of the Most High will overshadow you; therefore the child to be born will be holy; he will be called Son of God. . . . For nothing will be impossible with God." (Luke 1:35, 37)

**Reflection for younger children:** For St. Francis of Assisi, Christmas was the feast of feasts, the day when God, Creator of the world, was born a little babe. So a few weeks before Christmas in 1223, St. Francis told his friend, John Velita, that he wanted to celebrate the birth of Jesus on a hillside above John's town of Greccio. He also wanted to see before his eyes the discomforts our Savior endured in infancy. He asked his friend to set up a real manger with hay and to bring a donkey and an ox.

On Christmas Eve, in one long procession with torches held high to light the way, the village priest along with St. Francis, friars, villagers, and people from the surrounding country chanted hymns as they made their way up the hillside to the crib that was set up. The people gathered around as the priest began Mass, the torchlight glowing like a gigantic star.

St. Francis chanted the gospel. Then he preached on the joys awaiting those flocking to the babe of Bethlehem. And so it was that St. Francis created the first Christmas crèche. (Adapted from *St. Francis of Assisi: A Biography*. Used with permission of St. Anthony Messenger Press.)

## Fourth Sunday of Advent
## Year C
### MICAH 5:1-4   PSALM 80:2-3, 15-16, 18-19
### HEBREWS 10:5-10   LUKE 1:39-45

**Reading for older children:** And it is by God's will that we have been sanctified through the offering of the body of Jesus Christ once for all. (Hebrews 10:10)

**Reflection for older children:** In sixteenth-century England, Catholics could not openly practice their faith. If they were found with any written material that indicated they were Catholic, they could be imprisoned or hanged. Parents wanted their children to learn about their faith, especially that Jesus Christ offered his body on the tree of the cross for them. So someone made up an underground catechism similar to a child's counting song and called it "The Twelve Days of Christmas."

The song's gift for the first day of Christmas is a partridge in a pear tree, a secret code for Christ on the cross. A mother partridge lures a fox away from her nestlings by pretending to have a broken wing, thus saving their lives but giving up her own. The pear tree is the tree of the cross. We can thank our Father for Christ's offering on the cross whenever we hear or sing "The Twelve Days of Christmas."

**Reading for younger children:** "For as soon as I heard the sound of your greeting, the child in my womb leaped for joy. And blessed is she who believed that there would be a fulfillment of what was spoken to her by the Lord." (Luke 1:44-45)

**Reflection for younger children:** Mary and Elizabeth shared one another's joy in the coming birth of their babies. So did a mother and father who joyfully greeted the news that they were expecting their first child.

The baby girl, who was also the first grandchild, blessed the entire family. But when she was two months old, she became very pale and began having trouble breathing. Medical tests showed that she had cancer in her blood.

The doctor prescribed a drug for the baby. The father and mother prayed for the baby, and they asked everyone they knew to pray for her as well. They believed that the drug and the prayers would make her well. Two months later their prayers were answered: The cancer was gone. And everyone rejoiced once more.

# 3

# Reflections for Weekdays

# Prayers for the First Week of Advent

**Opening prayer:** All make the sign of the cross and say: "May we keep the Lord's words in our hearts and minds."

**Closing prayer:** "Father, open our eyes and hearts to ways we can love while we wait for Jesus."

**Response:** "Let us love while we wait for Jesus."

Or

**Sing:**   O come, O come Emmanuel,
And ransom captive Israel,
That mourns in lonely exile here,
Until the Son of God appear.
Rejoice! Rejoice! Emmanuel
Shall come to thee, O Israel.

End with an "Our Father."

# Monday of First Week

ISAIAH 2:1-5  PSALM 122:1-9  MATTHEW 8:5-11

**Reading for older children:** When [Jesus] entered Capernaum, a centurion came to him, appealing to him and saying, "Lord, my servant is lying at home paralyzed, in terrible distress." And he said to him, "I will come and cure him." The centurion answered, "Lord, I am not worthy to have you come under my roof; but only speak the word, and my servant will be healed. For I also am a man under authority, with soldiers under me; and I say to one, 'Go,' and he goes, and to another, 'Come,' and he comes, and to my slave, 'Do this,' and the slave does it." When Jesus heard him, he was amazed. (Matthew 8:5-10)

**Reflection for older children:** The centurion's faith was so strong that he believed Jesus could heal his servant, even if Jesus wasn't physically present. Like the centurion, a young widow named Susan had amazing faith.

Susan had two young sons, and earned a living by running a day care in her home. However, her house was in disrepair. It needed so much work that she just couldn't continue caring for children in that house. The problem was that she had no money to fix it up. She put it on the market, hoping to get enough money from the sale to buy a house in better condition, where she could continue her day care business. She and her little sons prayed in faith to the Lord for a solution.

After several months, someone made an offer—but it wasn't enough to buy the kind of house she needed. Susan turned it down, and she and her two sons continued to pray. A few weeks later, a new offer came in—for a lot more money! Susan was able to buy a good house where she could have her day care business. The new house was also close to many of her friends.

Like Susan and her two sons, we can have faith like the centurion, even when we're not sure how things will turn out.

**Reading for younger children:** For the sake of the house of the LORD our God, I will seek your good. (Psalm 122:9)

**Reflection for younger children:** God wants us to "seek good" for everyone, but especially for those in our family. To seek someone's good means that we want the best for them. Here's a story about a three-year-old girl named Bridget who wanted good things for her younger sister.

One day Bridget and her little sister Megan were visiting their grandmother and making Christmas cookies. Suddenly Megan fell off a chair. She cried and cried. The grandmother knew that Megan was not seriously hurt, but she wouldn't stop crying. When the grandmother tried to comfort her, Megan cried even harder.

Bridget said, "Grandma, Megan always cries like that when she's hurt. I know how we can help her! Jesus lives in our hearts, so we can ask him to take her hurts away and stop her crying."

So while Megan wailed, Bridget and her grandmother prayed with her. When they finished praying, Megan stopped crying, and they went back to making their cookies. Bridget was happy that she had helped her sister.

What is some "good" you can do for someone in your family today?

# Tuesday of First Week
ISAIAH 11:1-10 PSALM 72:1, 7-8, 12-13, 17 LUKE 10:21-24

**Reading for older children:** The wolf shall live with the lamb, the leopard shall lie down with the kid, the calf and the lion and the fatling together, and a little child shall lead them. The cow and the bear shall graze, their young shall lie down together; and the lion shall eat straw like the ox. . . . On that day the root of Jesse shall stand as a signal to the peoples; the nations shall inquire of him, and his dwelling shall be glorious. (Isaiah 11:6-7, 10)

**Reflection for older children:** One of the names for Jesus is the "Root of Jesse." So it is Jesus who stands as a signal—a signal of a new order, an order of love. The prophet Isaiah described this order when he said that the wolf would live with the lamb, and the cow and the bear would graze together. These descriptions are taken from nature to describe how radical this new order of love would be. How can we express this new order of love in our own lives?

St. Thérèse of Lisieux, who is called the Little Flower, thought she was too weak to do anything famous or noteworthy. So she prayed and discovered that her "little way" to God was to do each little thing with great love.

One of the Carmelite nuns at her monastery irritated Thérèse. Whenever Thérèse saw her, she wanted to run to another room. Then Thérèse thought: "This sister is God's creation. He loves his creation, so I must love her too." So Thérèse smiled every time she saw the sister. One day the sister asked, "What is it about me that pleases you so much, Sister Thérèse, since you always have a smile for me?"

Think of a way this week that you can express the new order of love in your family, like Thérèse did for the nun in her monastery.

*First Week of Advent* | 43

**Reading for younger children:** Jesus rejoiced in the Holy Spirit and said, "I thank you, Father, Lord of heaven and earth, because you have hidden these things from the wise and the intelligent and have revealed them to infants; yes, Father, for such was your gracious will." (Luke 10:21)

**Reflection for younger children:** Why was Jesus rejoicing? He had sent out seventy disciples to preach the good news. They were excited when they returned from the surrounding cities and towns. When they had called on the name of Jesus, they saw powerful things happen. Here were ordinary, uneducated people who saw God's power at work!

A person doesn't need a lot of education to understand the things of God. The fact is that the Holy Spirit reveals truth to hearts open to him, no matter what their age or education.

Once, when a four-year-old girl was waiting in the emergency room, a doctor asked her why she was so pretty. She replied, "It's because God made me." Her answer surprised the doctor, and he was quiet for a moment. Then he said, "Why, yes!" That day, the little girl revealed an important truth to the doctor: that God is the creator of all things.

Even though you are a child, remember that God can reveal his truth to you. He loves you and wants you to have a heart open to him. You too can see God's power at work in your life!

# Wednesday of First Week
ISAIAH 25:6-10   PSALM 23:1-6   MATTHEW 15:29-37

**Reading for older children:** The LORD is my shepherd, I shall not want. He makes me lie down in green pastures; he leads me beside still waters; he restores my soul. He leads me in right paths for his name's sake. Even though I walk through the darkest valley, I fear no evil; for you are with me; your rod and your staff—they comfort me. (Psalm 23:1-4)

**Reflection for older children:** Many people are afraid when they are facing death. They can be especially afraid if they have made bad choices in their lives that resulted in sin, and haven't yet asked God for forgiveness. Sometimes we need to tell others that it's never too late to be forgiven. Sometimes we need to be the comforting hand of God.

A seventy-year-old woman knew that her neighbor Mike was living an immoral lifestyle, but she was always pleasant to him. One day she noticed that he looked ill. Several months later, she heard that he was in the hospital, dying of complications from AIDS. She knew she should go visit him. Perhaps he needed comfort. Perhaps she could share the Lord's love with him.

The woman kept putting off the visit. Finally one day she felt she *had* to visit him *that* day. When she entered his hospital room, she was surprised by how sick he looked. His greeting was barely audible. She asked if he knew who she was, and he nodded.

Then she asked Mike if he knew that God loved him. He nodded yes. She asked him if he knew that God was merciful and forgiving. Again, he nodded. Then she took the young man's hand and prayed. "Father, be with Mike right now. Assure him of your love and forgiveness." As the woman continued to hold his hand, she prayed for him. Ten minutes later, Mike died.

**Reading for younger children:** It will be said on that day, Lo, this is our God; we have waited for him, so that he might save us. This is the LORD for whom we have waited; let us be glad and rejoice in his salvation. (Isaiah 25:9)

**Reflection for younger children:** Adam and Eve disobeyed God. Yet, he was their Father, and he still loved them. He told his people that he would send them a Savior to bring them back to him. They waited for many, many years. Then, sure enough, his Son Jesus was born of Mary.

Advent is a time for waiting. We know what we are waiting for—the baby Jesus! As we wait for Christmas to arrive, let's prepare our hearts to receive him. Jesus saved us by taking our sins to the cross. Now we can be glad and rejoice, because we can be forgiven.

You can prepare your heart this Advent by receiving forgiveness of your sins in the Sacrament of Reconciliation. If you haven't yet made your first Penance, you can still prepare your heart by praying to God and asking him to forgive you for anything you have done wrong. You can also ask forgiveness of any person you have wronged. Just think how ready you'll be when it's time to sing "Happy Birthday" to Jesus!

# Thursday of First Week
ISAIAH 26:1-6  PSALM 118:1, 8-9, 19-21, 25-27
MATTHEW 7:21, 24-27

**Reading for older children:** "Not everyone who says to me, 'Lord, Lord,' will enter the kingdom of heaven, but only the one who does the will of my Father in heaven." (Matthew 7:21)

**Reflection for older children:** Sometimes we know what God's will is for our life, but are afraid to do it. Joe was ready to graduate from high school. He thought that the Lord was calling him to serve the poor that summer. Joe wanted to do God's will, but he didn't know how he could serve the poor and still work at a summer job. He needed the money from his job in order to go to college in the fall.

Joe was afraid that God was asking him to do something he couldn't do. So he talked with his parents. They said he shouldn't be afraid. If Joe followed the Lord's call, he could trust that his heavenly Father would work out the details. Joe was able to find a paid summer job—working with the poor! Joe worked all summer at a city recreation center in a poor neighborhood. He met many boys and girls from poor families, and had many opportunities to help and encourage them. After the summer was over, he had enough money to start college.

Have you ever been afraid to do God's will because you saw so many obstacles in the way? Were you surprised by how God worked things out?

**Reading for younger children:** The LORD is God, and he has given us light. (Psalm 118:27)

**Reflection for younger children:** Jesus is the light of the world, and when we pray for him to be the light in our lives, he will answer our prayers.

Every morning Sarah prayed: "The thoughts in my mind, the love in my heart, the works of my hands, I offer to you, dear Jesus." One morning, after Sarah had said this prayer, her grandmother asked the little girl to get a sweater for her. Sarah was playing a video game and didn't want to be interrupted. Then, it was as if a light went on in her heart. She remembered her morning prayer and decided to love her grandmother as Jesus would. She got up from her game to get the sweater.

You can pray that Jesus will light up your heart each day with his love. Then, during the day, look for times when God is asking you to show his light to others.

# Friday of First Week
ISAIAH 29:17-24   PSALM 27:1, 4, 13-14   MATTHEW 9:27-31

**Reading for older children:** Wait for the LORD; be strong, and let your heart take courage; wait for the LORD! (Psalm 27:14)

**Reflection for older children:** No one likes to wait, but Scripture tells us that we should wait on the Lord. We have to be strong and courageous and patient while we wait—all the while asking God to answer our prayer!

One family prayed for many years for their father to be healed of a debilitating disease. The man became so weak that he had to quit his job. Finally, the doctors said there was no hope:

His heart, lungs, and kidneys were failing. Everyone at the hospital expected him to die shortly.

While he was in the hospital, a nurse's aide came into his room. She said to him: "Don't be afraid. Jesus is with you, healing you. Be patient." Later a priest anointed him and sensed that God was healing him. Several men prayed with him, and again sensed that he would be healed. After eleven days of slow recovery, he had a chest scan. The scan showed that his lungs were in perfect condition! That was six years ago, and this husband and father of five is still telling everyone his story. After so many years of waiting on the Lord, he was healed of his disease.

Is there a situation in your life where you need to be strong in your faith and wait for the Lord?

**Reading for younger children:** When he entered the house, the blind men came to him; and Jesus said to them, "Do you believe that I am able to do this?" They said to him, "Yes, Lord." Then he touched their eyes and said, "According to your faith let it be done to you." (Matthew 9:28-29)

**Reflection for younger children:** The gospels are filled with many stories of Jesus healing people. But do you know that Jesus can still heal people today? Here's a modern-day healing story.

For many months a little boy named Brendan had painful stomach aches and diarrhea after eating. Brendan's doctor tried different diets and medicine, but nothing helped. Then the doctor ordered special tests. The tests showed that he might have a serious disease. The doctor told his parents to take Brendan to a specialist at a children's hospital.

Before the appointment, the boy's family and friends prayed with him. They believed that God would heal him. Gradually the stomach aches and diarrhea stopped. When he went to the children's hospital, the specialist said Brendan was fine. Everyone rejoiced that the boy was healed.

Do you know someone who needs healing? Pray to Jesus to heal that person, just like he did this little boy.

## Saturday of First Week
ISAIAH 30:19-21, 23-26  PSALM 147:1-6
MATTHEW 9:35–10:1, 6-8

**Reading for older children:** He will surely be gracious to you at the sound of your cry; when he hears it, he will answer you. (Isaiah 30:19)

**Reflection for older children:** The Lord listens to the cries of our heart, often through the people he sends our way.

One day a sales clerk was ringing up the purchases of a customer. All the while, she was complaining about the pain in her back. The clerk said her neighbor had left a large, heavy car battery in her yard. When she carried it back to her neighbor's yard, she had injured her back. The clerk didn't stop complaining until she handed the receipt to the customer.

The customer gently touched the clerk's hand and said, "I'll pray for your back to be healed, and that things will go better with your neighbor."

The sales clerk looked stunned. "I need to forgive my neighbor, don't I?" She didn't wait for an answer. "I believe God sent you to me today!"

Do you remember a time when you were able to hear someone's "cry" and comfort them with an encouraging word? God can use you in many situations to be a "sounding board" for others!

**Reading for younger children:** Then he said to his disciples, "The harvest is plentiful, but the laborers are few; therefore ask the Lord of the harvest to send out laborers into his harvest. . . . As you go, proclaim the good news, 'The kingdom of heaven has come near.' " (Matthew 9:37-38; 10:7)

**Reflection for younger children:** The disciples were sent out to proclaim the good news. We are disciples of Jesus, so how do we proclaim the good news?

Here's what two sisters did. A new girl in the neighborhood, who was called Jenny, came over to play. They asked her to stay for lunch. When it was time to eat their peanut butter sandwiches, the two sisters prayed and asked Jesus to bless their lunch. Jenny asked them why they said those words. The sisters discovered that Jenny had never heard much about Jesus. So they told her all about him. After a few weeks, she went to Mass with them. After a few more weeks, her mother went to Mass with them, too.

Proclaiming the good news is nothing more than telling people about Jesus!

# Prayers for the Second Week of Advent

Light two purple candles this week.

**Opening prayer:** All make the sign of the cross and say: "May we keep the Lord's words in our hearts and minds."

**Closing prayer:** "Father, give us strength for doing good so we can prepare the way for Christ Jesus."

**Closing response:** "Jesus is coming! Prepare the way for the Lord!"

Or

**Sing:**   O Come, thou wisdom from on high,
Who orders all things mightily,
To us the path of knowledge show,
And teach us in her ways to go.
Rejoice! Rejoice! Emmanuel
Shall come to thee, O Israel.

End with an "Our Father."

# Monday of Second Week
ISAIAH 35:1-10   PSALM 85:9-14   LUKE 5:17-26

**Reading for older children:** Strengthen the weak hands, and make firm the feeble knees. Say to those who are of fearful heart, "Be strong, do not fear! Here is your God. . . . He will come and save you." (Isaiah 35:3-4)

**Reflection for older children:** Often fear can paralyze us. But the opposite of fear is love. When we realize how much God loves us, we can let go of our fears. Here's how a nurse helped her patient conquer fear.

An elderly hospital patient was suddenly seized with a fear of being poisoned. For several days, she refused to leave her hospital room, talk with anyone, or eat. A psychiatric nurse came to see her and introduced herself, explaining that she wanted to help her. Filled with fear, the patient acted as if the nurse were not in the room. Not knowing what to do, the nurse left the room and prayed.

Then she remembered seeing a well-worn Bible lying open on the patient's nightstand. The nurse wrote on a piece of paper: "Who will separate us from the love of Christ? . . . For I am convinced that neither death, nor life, nor angels, nor rulers, nor things present, nor things to come, nor powers, nor height, nor depth, nor anything else in all creation, will be able to separate us from the love of God in Christ Jesus our Lord" (Romans 8:35, 38-39). She left the passage on the patient's nightstand.

The patient found the note and read it. Within a few hours, she left her room, found the nurse, and talked with her for the rest of the day. Then she ate her dinner. She had been freed from her fear.

**Reading for younger children:** Just then some men came, carrying a paralyzed man on a bed. They were trying to bring him in and lay him before Jesus; but finding no way to bring him in because of the crowd, they went up on the roof and let him down with his bed through the tiles into the middle of the crowd in front of Jesus. When he saw their faith, he said, "Friend, your sins are forgiven you. . . . Which is easier, to say, 'Your sins are forgiven you,' or to say, 'Stand up and walk'? But so that you may know that the Son of Man has authority on earth to forgive sins"—he said to the one who was paralyzed—"I say to you, stand up and take your bed and go to your home." Immediately he stood up . . . and went home, glorifying God. (Luke 5:18-20, 23-25)

**Reflection for younger children:** Having our sins forgiven is as amazing as having a paralyzed man walk. Here's the story of one little girl who was forgiven.

Karen's mother had baked some cookies to give to a family with a new baby. Before she could give them away, however, the cookies disappeared. When her mother asked Karen what had happened to them, she looked guilty and lied, telling her that she didn't know. Gently, her mother helped her to tell the truth.

Karen asked to be forgiven for eating the cookies and for lying about it. Her mother forgave her and gave Karen a hug. Together they went to the grocery store to buy cookies to give to the family, using Karen's money to pay for them. Karen was glad that her mother had forgiven her, and she knew that God had forgiven her too. Like the friends of the paralyzed man, this mother helped her daughter to experience the mercy of God.

# Tuesday of Second Week
Isaiah 40:1-11   Psalm 96:1-3, 10-13   Matthew 18:12-14

**Reading for older children:** "If a shepherd has a hundred sheep, and one of them has gone astray, does he not leave the ninety-nine on the mountains and go in search of the one that went astray? . . . So it is not the will of your Father in heaven that one of these little ones should be lost." (Matthew 18:12, 14)

**Reflection for older children:** We all stray sometimes. When we do, God goes in search of us. That's how much he loves us and wants us to be with him.

In the Basilica of the Sacred Heart on the campus of the University of Notre Dame in Indiana, there is a small stained glass window that could go unnoticed. However, if you wait in line to go to the Sacrament of Reconciliation, you face it. A little lamb is so entangled in a thornbush that he cannot escape. But Jesus is pulling apart the thorny branches to free him.

Often we feel entangled by our sins. Sometimes we feel hopelessly lost. But Jesus is waiting to free us in the Sacrament of Reconciliation. When you celebrate this sacrament, think of Jesus seeking you out and then untangling you from your sins. That's why he came into the world on Christmas—to free all of us from our sins so that we could live with God forever.

**Reading for younger children:** O sing to the LORD a new song; sing to the LORD, all the earth. Sing to the LORD, bless his name; tell of his salvation from day to day. (Psalm 96:1-2)

**Reflection for younger children:** How can you bless God's name, as the psalm says? One of the ways to bless God's name is to thank him and praise him.

At night before falling asleep, think of five things that God has done for you during the day. Then thank the Lord for them. Perhaps you wanted to do or say something wrong and you didn't—that was your heavenly Father helping you. You could thank him for the fun you had playing with a friend, for the good-tasting food you ate at dinner, or for understanding a difficult math problem.

When we remember to thank God for all his gifts, we are blessing God—but he also blesses us! Every time we pray, we are blessed, because when we talk to God, we get to know him better, and he becomes our very best friend!

## Wednesday of Second Week
ISAIAH 40:25-31   PSALM 103:1-4, 8, 10   MATTHEW 11:28-30

**Reading for older children:** Have you not known? Have you not heard? The LORD is the everlasting God, the Creator of the ends of the earth. He does not faint or grow weary; his understanding is unsearchable. He gives power to the faint, and strengthens the powerless. (Isaiah 40:28-29)

**Reflection for older children:** When we face difficulties, it can be hard to persevere—especially if we try to go it alone, without asking the Lord for help. But when we ask God to give us *his* strength, we can endure.

Jay, a high school senior and captain of his soccer team, had applied to a military academy. However, before his entrance interview, he seriously injured his leg in a soccer game. The doctor gave him two alternatives. He could give up soccer for the rest of the season and work with a physical therapist, which would be a long and painful process. Or, he could have an operation and play. Jay knew that if he had the operation, the military academy would probably not accept him. He decided to work with the therapist.

For months he endured long hours of painful therapy. When he went to the interview, he had only a slight limp. Jay was accepted, and thanked God for the strength and power to persevere.

**Reading for younger children:** The Lord is merciful and gracious, slow to anger and abounding in steadfast love. He does not deal with us according to our sins, nor repay us according to our iniquities. (Psalm 103:8, 10)

**Reflection for younger children:** Oftentimes we learn about God's mercy through the mercy of others, especially our parents.

For several afternoons John came home late from school. His worried parents told him to come home right after school, or he would have bread and water for dinner. But he was late again.

That night for dinner, John watched his father help himself to large servings of chicken, mashed potatoes, gravy, and corn. The boy looked down at the slice of white bread on his plate. Then he watched in surprise as his father took away the plate with the slice of bread on it and exchanged it for the plate heaped with food.

The boy knew he deserved bread and water for dinner, and that his father was being merciful to him by not carrying out the punishment for his disobedience. This act of mercy helped him to understand how our heavenly Father "does not deal with us according to our sins," but is merciful and abounding in steadfast love.

## Thursday of Second Week
ISAIAH 41:13-20   PSALM 145:1, 9-13   MATTHEW 11:11-15

**Reading for older children:** The LORD is good to all, and his compassion is over all that he has made. (Psalm 145:9)

**Reflection for older children:** We often think we have to be good in order for God to love us. But we can't earn God's love. He loves us unconditionally, even when we are knowingly doing wrong.

One young woman named Bonnie had been raised in a faith-filled Catholic family, but when she turned eighteen, she wanted to leave home. She moved out of her house and into a trailer with her boyfriend. One day Bonnie received a package from her father. In it was a Bible, along with a note saying he hoped she would come to know the Lord and change her life.

A few weeks later, the young couple returned to discover that a fire had destroyed their trailer. A firefighter walked with the woman through the inside of the charred trailer. Under a pile of burnt papers was the Bible. It had not even been scorched.

Bonnie knew that God had preserved the Bible for a reason. She understood God's compassion. He had loved her even while she was living an immoral lifestyle. She knew it was time for change. She broke up with her boyfriend, moved back home, and started to read the Bible that God had saved for her.

**Reading for younger children:** For I, the LORD your God, hold your right hand; it is I who say to you, "Do not fear, I will help you." . . . When the poor and needy seek water, and there is none, and their tongue is parched with thirst . . . I the God of Israel will not forsake them. (Isaiah 41:13, 17)

**Reflection for younger children:** As followers of Jesus, we are called to care for those who have less than we do. Some people are hungry because they have no food. Some people are cold because they have no heat. When we see others in need, we should help them.

One very cold winter day, the local newspaper featured an article about a family with small children who could not pay their gas bill. A photo showed a grandmother, who lived with the family, wrapping the children in blankets to keep them warm. Even though the children's mother had gone to the gas company to tell them that they had no money to pay the bill, the company would not turn on the heat.

At breakfast that morning, a couple in another part of the same city read the article. They wanted to help. They went to the gas company and paid the family's gas bill, because they knew that God wanted them to care for those in need.

This Advent, look for an opportunity to help someone in need. Whatever you do, even if it is something small, will be pleasing to God if it is done with love.

# Friday of Second Week
ISAIAH 48:17-19  PSALM 1:1-4, 6  MATTHEW 11:16-19

**Reading for older children:** Draw near to me, hear this! From the beginning I have not spoken in secret, from the time it came to be I have been there. And now the Lord GOD has sent me and his spirit. Thus says the LORD, your Redeemer, the Holy One of Israel: I am the LORD your God, who teaches you for your own good, who leads you in the way you should go. (Isaiah 48:16-17)

**Reflection for older children:** When we are going the wrong way, God tries to show us the right way. Sometimes he is very direct!

Every Monday night at her parish, a grandmother prayed a novena to the Blessed Mother for her husband to come back to the Catholic Church. He had not been to Mass in many years.

One day the grandfather was reading the newspaper after work when he heard a voice say, "Joe, I want you to come back to the Church." He laughed, thinking someone was playing a practical joke. He looked through the house, but no one was there. Puzzled he sat down again and picked up the newspaper. Again the voice said, "Joe, I want you to come back to the Church."

When his wife returned from work, he told her about the voice he had heard and asked her what he should do. She suggested he go talk to their pastor. Several hours later, he returned. He had gone to confession for the first time in forty years. From then on, he faithfully went to Mass. For the rest of his life, he never forgot that God had spoken to him and led him in the way he should go.

**Reading for younger children:** The LORD watches over the way of the righteous. (Psalm 1:6)

**Reflection for younger children:** Being "righteous" means doing the right thing. Many times each day, we are given a choice. We can choose to do what is right, or we can choose to do what is wrong.

A girl found a bracelet in the school restroom. It was a beautiful bracelet, and no one saw her pick it up. She could have kept it, and no one would have known. But she turned it into the school office, and its owner was found.

Think of a time this past week when you had a choice about whether to do the right thing or the wrong thing. Did you make the right choice? If not, what would have helped you to make a better choice?

## Saturday of Second Week
SIRACH 48:1-4, 9-11  PSALM 80:2-3, 15-16, 18-19
MATTHEW 17:10-13

**Reading for older children:** "But I tell you that Elijah has already come, and they did not recognize him, but they did to him whatever they pleased. So also the Son of Man is about to suffer at their hands." (Matthew 17:12)

**Reflection for older children:** Blessed Mother Teresa often said that Christ can be found in the "distressing disguise of the poor." She would tell others that if they wanted to see Christ, they should look for him in those who are suffering and most in need.

A woman who visits a nursing home sees Christ suffering in the residents there. The residents cannot care for themselves. Many can't feed or dress themselves, get out of bed, go to the bathroom without help, or sit up. Some cry out in pain. Many do not talk. Most use wheelchairs.

But unlike Christ who suffered at the hands of others, the hands of the caregivers ease the suffering of the residents. They bathe them, shampoo and cut their hair, dress them, help them eat, and greet them with cheerful hellos. They decorate the halls for holidays. They provide dogs for the residents to pet, puppies to hold, and a large cage with brightly colored birds. There is a chapel for Mass, prayer, and a weekly rosary.

Christ is in the suffering, but he is also in the hands that relieve the suffering. Perhaps during this Advent season, you can visit a nursing home with your family or youth group. You might play cards with one of the residents or sing Christmas carols for them. As you do so, you will recognize Christ in the faces of the residents, and they will recognize Christ in you.

**Reading for younger children:** Stir up your might, and come to save us! Restore us, O God; let your face shine, that we may be saved. (Psalm 80:2-3)

**Reflection for younger children:** When the Hebrews found themselves in tough situations, they would pray for God to save them. When we are in tough situations, we can do the same thing. God is mighty, and he can save us.

As a mother sat nervously outside the Catholic school principal's office, she prayed to God for help. Both her salary and her husband's had been cut, and they needed two thousand dollars to cover the tuition for their three children. She asked the Lord to help her find the money so that her children could stay at the school.

The principal's door opened, and a couple who had been talking with the principal left. The sister welcomed the young mother. As she began to explain her situation, she broke down in tears.

"Oh, my dear, don't worry," the sister said kindly. "The couple before you just gave us a two thousand-dollar donation that was unexpected. Now it's yours. Our God provides!"

# Prayers for the Third Week of Advent

Light two purple candles and one pink or white candle this week.

**Opening prayer:** All make the sign of the cross and say: "May we keep the Lord's words in our hearts and minds."

**Closing prayer:** "Father, give us new zeal to love others. Let us rejoice as we eagerly await the coming of Jesus."

**Response:** "Rejoice! Jesus is coming soon! Let us love with new zeal as we eagerly wait for him."

Or

**Sing:** O come, O come, thou Lord of Might,
Who to the tribes on Sinai's height
In ancient times did give the law,
In power, majesty and awe.
Rejoice! Rejoice! Emmanuel
Shall come to thee, O Israel.

End with an "Our Father."

# Monday of Third Week

NUMBERS 24:2-7, 15-17  PSALM 25:4-9  MATTHEW 21:23-27

**Reading for older children:** When [Jesus] entered the temple, the chief priests and the elders of the people came to him as he was teaching, and said, "By what authority are you doing these things, and who gave you this authority?" (Matthew 21:23)

**Reflection for older children:** Jesus was the Son of God. His authority came from his Father in heaven. If the chief priests and elders acknowledged that Jesus' authority came directly from God, they would have had to change their hearts and do what Jesus said.

God gave Jesus authority over everything in heaven and on earth (Matthew 28:18). Sometimes the Lord delegates his authority to his people. For example, your parents have authority over you until you are old enough to live on your own. That authority is a gift, because it means that your parents care for you and want the best for you. They are responsible for what happens to you. Sometimes you may not want to listen to them, but their authority is from God. When you obey them, you are also obeying God.

Sometimes it's difficult to see parental authority as a gift. As Christmas approaches, ask the Lord to help you appreciate your parents and their care for you. Ask God to give you a heart ready and willing to obey.

**Reading for younger children:** Make me to know your ways, O LORD; teach me your paths. (Psalm 25:4)

**Reflection for younger children:** Our ways are not always the Lord's ways. Sometimes the Lord wants us to put aside our own desires so that we can help others. For example, one morning a mother was rushing to complete her speed-walking exercise when she saw an older man slowly shuffling along, squarely in her path. She thought: "I don't have time to be neighborly. I'll keep walking. He'll understand." But she slowed down and nodded to him.

"Do you mind if I walk with you?" he asked.

"I'm walking pretty fast," she answered.

"That's okay. I probably couldn't keep up." He was clearly disappointed.

The woman knew the Lord's way would be to walk with the man. So she slowed down to accompany him. While they walked, the neighbor asked her to pray for him so that he would be healed from the effects of a stroke. Right then and there, they prayed. This mom was very glad she had taken the time to talk to her neighbor.

## Tuesday of Third Week
ZEPHANIAH 3:1-2, 9-13   PSALM 34:2-3, 6-7, 17-19, 23
MATTHEW 21:28-32

**Reading for older children:** [Jerusalem] has listened to no voice; it has accepted no correction. It has not trusted in the LORD; it has not drawn near to its God. (Zephaniah 3:2)

**Reflection for older children:** It's often hard to trust in the Lord, especially when we think we know better. But not listening to the Lord can have dire consequences.

Have you ever heard of this modern-day "parable" of a mountain climber who failed to listen to God's instructions? He set out alone, and was making good time. However, when he was only a few feet from the top, it started to snow very hard, and he slipped. Falling through the air at great speed, he knew he was close to death. Then the rope he had tied around his waist jerked him. His body dangled in midair. He realized the rope was holding him. He screamed, "Help me, God."

A voice answered, "What do you want?"

The climber said, "Save me!"

"Do you really believe I can save you?" asked the voice.

"Yes!" the climber replied.

"Then cut the rope around your waist."

Not trusting in the Lord, the climber held onto the rope with all his strength. The next day a rescue team found him, frozen and dead, holding tightly to the rope only ten feet from the ground.

Think of a time when you were tempted not to trust in the Lord. What was the result?

**Reading for younger children:** [Jesus said:] "What do you think? A man had two sons; he went to the first and said, 'Son, go and work in the vineyard today.' He answered, 'I will not'; but later he changed his mind and went.

The father went to the second and said the same; and he answered, 'I go, sir'; but he did not go. Which of the two did the will of his father?" They said, "The first." Jesus said to them, "Truly I tell you, the tax collectors and the prostitutes are going into the kingdom of God ahead of you." (Matthew 21:28-31)

**Reflection for younger children:** Have you ever been given a second chance to do the right thing, even when you may have done the wrong thing the first time around? That's what happened to the first son in Jesus' story. He said no to his father's request, but then realized that he had disobeyed his father. He had a second chance to go into the vineyard to work, and he did.

The sinners in Jesus' day were also given a second chance. They had chosen to do many bad things, but Jesus was telling them that it was not too late! They could still choose the right thing, and they would be doing what God wanted. God always gives us a second chance, because he's always willing to forgive us for our sins. In fact, after Adam and Eve turned away from God, the Father sent Jesus into the world to give all of us a second chance! Even if we've made bad choices in the past, we can do the right thing today.

## Wednesday of Third Week
ISAIAH 45:6-8, 18, 21-25   PSALM 85:9-14   LUKE 7:18-23

**Reading for older children:** The LORD will give what is good, and our land will yield its increase. (Psalm 85:12)

**Reflection for older children:** Do you believe that God will give good things to those who ask him? A single mother with six children wanted to buy a newly constructed house, but she earned too little to get a loan.

One of the men from a Christian group that had helped to build the house went to a bank and told the loan officer about the work the group was doing. They had wanted to show their love to that family and others in the neighborhood by building new houses.

The loan officer was touched—and wanted to help. She said, "Bring all your loans to me. This is what gives purpose to my job." The single mom was able to get the loan and the house! The Lord gave "what is good" to that family with six children.

**Reading for younger children:** In the LORD all the offspring of Israel shall triumph and glory. (Isaiah 45:25)

**Reflection for younger children:** "Offspring" means a child—sons and daughters just like you! Parents want their children to believe in God, and to live in a way that gives glory to him.

Here's how one family glorified God. The Grants were known in the neighborhood for their hospitality. However, one of the neighbors on the street, Hank, complained about all the noise and activity at their house. The Grants heard his complaints for many years. Then one day they found out that Hank had cancer.

A few days before Christmas, Hank's wife called the Grants, saying that her husband wondered if their family would come and sing "O Little Town of Bethlehem" for him on Christmas Day.

All twenty-one of the Grants—grandparents, parents, teens, and toddlers—sang carols for him. Here was a family glorifying God by showing their love to a neighbor in need. The family continued to visit him, as did relatives and the priest from the nearby parish. Before he died, Hank told the Grants how grateful he was for their visits.

# Thursday of Third Week
ISAIAH 54:1-10   PSALM 30:2, 4-6, 11-13   LUKE 7:24-30

**Reading for older children:** O LORD my God, I cried to you for help, and you have healed me. . . . Sing praises to the LORD, O you his faithful ones, and give thanks to his holy name. (Psalm 30:2, 4)

**Reflection for older children:** Sometimes we have to hit "rock bottom" before we realize we need God and cry out to him for help. This is what happened to one young man who was addicted to drugs and alcohol.

David had been imprisoned for shoplifting when he was still a senior in high school. After he was released from jail, he traveled all over the country, selling drugs to support his addiction. When he was twenty, he was befriended by a young woman whose parents allowed him to live in their basement bedroom. The father tried to help David by making appointments for him at a drug treatment center.

When the young woman left home to take a job out of the state, David became angry with God because he realized that he loved her. It was the first time he had ever acknowledged that God existed or that he loved anyone. Then he cried out to God to heal his addictions. Gradually he was no longer tempted by drugs or alcohol.

When David asked God what he wanted from him, he heard the word "perseverance." So he persevered in staying away from drugs and alcohol. He found a job and eventually married the young woman. Like the psalmist, David still gives thanks to God for healing him and giving him a new life.

**Reading for younger children:** Jesus began to speak to the crowds about John: "What did you go out into the wilderness to look at? A reed shaken by the wind? What then did you go out to see? Someone dressed in soft robes? Look, those who put on fine clothing and live in luxury are in royal palaces. What then did you go out to see? A prophet? Yes, I tell you, and more than a prophet. This is the one about whom it is written, 'See, I am sending my messenger ahead of you, who will prepare your way before you.' " (Luke 7:24-27)

**Reflection for younger children:** John the Baptist was no ordinary man. He lived in the wilderness, dressed in clothing made of camel hair, and ate locusts and wild honey. Many people came to hear him preach and to be baptized in the Jordan. They wanted to be cleansed of their sins.

John had a very special role to play. He was making hearts ready for the coming of Jesus. He would tell people: "Repent, for the kingdom of heaven has come near" (Matthew 3:2). When people listened to John, they recognized the sins in their lives and asked God to forgive them.

John once said that he was not worthy to untie Jesus' sandals. He knew he was only the messenger, not the savior. But Jesus said he was a great man. John did exactly what God wanted: He prepared the way for Jesus.

# Friday of Third Week
ISAIAH 56:1-3, 6-8   PSALM 67:2-3, 5, 7-8   JOHN 5:33-36

**Reading for older children:** "The works that the Father has given me to complete, the very works that I am doing, testify on my behalf that the Father has sent me." (John 5:36)

**Reflection for older children:** The Jewish leaders were suspicious of Jesus. How could he call God his own father? What evidence was there to support his claim?

First Jesus pointed to John the Baptist, who testified to the truth of who Jesus was. But beyond that, Jesus pointed to the works he had done. These miracles showed that God, his Father, was working through him.

The first part of John's Gospel is often called the "Book of Signs." Through signs like changing water into wine and healing the blind, Jesus sought to draw people to him. Even today, such "signs" are evidence that Jesus is alive and that he still works in power in the world. They are also evidence that we have a Father in heaven who loves us and wants to save us.

Today with your family, share some signs of God's love. It can be something simple, like the way he provides food and shelter for you, or something more dramatic, like the way he healed you or someone you know.

**Reading for younger children:** Thus says the Lord GOD . . . I will gather others to them besides those already gathered. (Isaiah 56:8)

**Reflection for younger children:** God wants everyone to become his sons and daughters. He wants people from every nation, from every race, and from every part of the world to know how wonderful he is.

St. Francis Xavier knew of God's desire to have everyone know and love him. When he was a young man, he left Europe, where he lived, to go to Asia. First he went to India, then to Malaysia, and then to Japan. He worked very hard telling people about Jesus. Many became believers.

Francis really wanted to go to China to spread the good news, but at that time, the Chinese government did not let foreigners into the country. So he planned for a trader to smuggle him in. As he waited on an island off the coast of China for the trader to pick him up, he came down with a fever and died. But the seeds he planted grew. Because of his work, many people came to Christ. He is one of the greatest missionaries the Church has ever known.

# Prayers for the Fourth Week of Advent

(Note: This begins the second part of Advent. From December 17 until Christmas, find the appropriate readings by following the calendar date.)

**Opening prayer:** All make the sign of the cross and say: "May we keep the Lord's words in our hearts and minds."

**Closing prayer:** "Our Christ is near. Let him find us loving one another when he comes."

**Response:** "Come, Lord Jesus, Come quickly!"

Or

**Sing:**    O come, thou Rod of Jesse's stem,
From every foe deliver them
That trust thy mighty power to save,
And give them vic'try o'er the grave.
Rejoice! Rejoice! Emmanuel
Shall come to thee, O Israel.

End with an "Our Father."

# December 17

Genesis 49:2, 8-10 Psalm 72:1-4, 7-8, 17 Matthew 1:1-17

**Reading for older children:** The scepter shall not depart from Judah, nor the ruler's staff from between his feet, until tribute comes to him; and the obedience of the peoples is his. (Genesis 49:10)

**Reflection for older children:** The scepter is the sign of one who rules. A ruler can rule by force, or he can rule as Jesus does, bringing about a whole new order in which people obey out of love.

Mr. Foster became the manager of a factory that had many problems. The previous factory manager had been difficult and confrontational. Disputes were frequently settled by fistfights. Discord ruled all relationships, not love.

At his first meeting, Mr. Foster told the employees that he wouldn't tolerate gossip, vulgarity, or hostility between workers. He said his door would always be open if an employee wanted to discuss a problem.

Over time, the atmosphere in the factory improved. Employees began to understand what was expected of them. People acted more kindly to one another. A year later, the factory celebrated record-breaking profits, and everyone received a raise. The rule Mr. Foster had brought to the factory was not one of force, but one of love. And love is always more powerful.

**Reading for younger children:** May he defend the cause of the poor of the people, give deliverance to the needy, and crush the oppressor. (Psalm 72:4)

**Reflection for younger children:** Many families have special traditions at Christmastime, like the Advent wreath and the Christmas tree. Some families also start their own Advent traditions that help the poor, like making food baskets or purchasing toys for children who have a parent in prison. Here's how one tradition got started among a group of teens and adults who go on a yearly mission trip to Mexico.

Every summer, these teens and adults visit a Mexican village and the outlying ranches of poor farmers. They help repair buildings and give away toys and treats.

One year, when the group was visiting a farm, one of the adults noticed that the old man who lived there was wearing tattered, homemade sandals. He immediately took off his shoes and gave them to the old man. The others followed his example, giving away their shoes and clothing. That day a new tradition was born. Every summer those going on this mission trip take along extra shoes and clothing to give away.

What tradition can your family begin this Advent to help the needy?

## December 18

JEREMIAH 23:5-8    PSALM 72:1-2, 12-13, 18-19    MATTHEW 1:18-25

**Reading for older children:** Now the birth of Jesus the Messiah took place in this way. When his mother Mary had been engaged to Joseph, but before they lived together, she was found to be with child from the Holy Spirit. . . . All this took place to fulfill what had been spoken by the Lord through the prophet: "Look, the virgin shall conceive and bear a son, and they shall name him Emmanuel," which means, "God is with us." (Matthew 1:18, 22-23)

**Reflection for older children:** God became flesh, and he dwelt among us. And even though Jesus no longer is here on earth in the flesh, his incarnation is for all time. He has never left us.

How does God dwell among us? A call went out to a parish community. After a young mother had delivered her fourth child, a nurse found her in a coma. She had a brain aneurysm and was taken to surgery. The priest decided that the parish should pray until God healed her.

The church was crowded. People were standing in the back and in the side aisles. The pastor was kneeling in the front, leading the prayers. Parishioners prayed around the clock. As one or two people left, others came to take their places. The prayer vigil ended when the woman was successfully wheeled out of surgery. It took several months for the mother to speak normally and to see well, but she and her family were overwhelmed by the love and constant prayer that had been offered on their behalf. The entire parish experienced "God is with us."

**Reading for younger children:** For he delivers the needy when they call, the poor and those who have no helper. He has pity on the weak and the needy, and saves the lives of the needy. (Psalm 72:12-13)

**Reflection for younger children:** After Pope John Paul II said Mass in Roznava, Slovakia, as part of his twenty-fifth anniversary tour, five-year-old twin girls went up to him where he sat in front of the altar receiving people. Their mother explained that the twins had been born joined at the hip but were separated by an operation. He tenderly stroked each girl on the cheek, then turned to the crowd and said, "Be protectors of life."

The pope's prayer is that the world would cherish the sacredness of life and protect the unborn and elderly. These are "the weak and the needy" who often "have no helper." If Jesus was willing to come into the world as a weak and helpless newborn baby, think about how much he wants us to treasure the gift of life, especially the lives of those who are helpless and in need of our protection.

# December 19
JUDGES 13:2-7, 24-25   PSALM 71:3-6, 16-17   LUKE 1:5-25

**Reading for older children:** Rescue me, O my God . . . For you, O Lord, are my hope, my trust, O LORD, from my youth. (Psalm 71:4-5)

**Reflection for older children:** Jesus was born to give us hope in time of trouble. Even when things are difficult, Jesus can give us hope and rescue us from our bitterness and anger.

St. Elizabeth Ann Seton was born in New York City in 1774. When she was fourteen, her father, Dr. Richard Bayley, and her stepmother could not agree on important issues and decided to live apart. Her father had no room for Elizabeth in his living quarters, and Mrs. Bayley had her hands full with eight children of her own. So for almost five years, Elizabeth lived with her married sister or an aunt, depending on who could take her at the time. Although she felt abandoned, Elizabeth did not grow bitter or lose hope. Instead, she spent her days praying the psalms in order to stay close to her heavenly Father.

Her hope and trust in the Lord began in her youth, and carried her through many difficult trials when she became an adult. When she was twenty-nine, she lost her husband to tuberculosis and had to support five young children on her own. When she converted to Catholicism, she was ostracized by many family members and friends. After she started her own religious order of nuns, the Sisters of Charity, two of her daughters died. Through it all she maintained her peace and trust in God.

**Reading for younger children:** But the angel said to him, "Do not be afraid, Zechariah, for your prayer has been heard. Your wife Elizabeth will bear you a son, and you will name him John." (Luke 1:13)

**Reflection for younger children:** All of their lives Zechariah and Elizabeth obeyed and loved God. And all their lives they prayed for a son. But they were old, past the age for having children.

Then one day an angel appeared to Zechariah with good news. God heard their prayer, and they would have a son. They should name him John. He would prepare God's people to get ready for the Lord.

Instead of thanking God for his awesome gift, Zechariah doubted that God could do this for an old man and woman. Because he didn't believe God could accomplish this wonderful thing, the angel took away Zechariah's speech. Still, God was true to his promise. Elizabeth conceived a child. After the child was born, Zechariah was able to speak again. He and Elizabeth thanked God for this great gift.

Sometimes we can doubt what God can do for us. When we do, we should remember how faithful God is and what he has done for us in the past. Then we can be confident of his plan for us for the future.

# December 20
ISAIAH 7:10-14   PSALM 24:1-6   LUKE 1:26-38

**Reading for older children:** Those who have clean hands and pure hearts . . . Such is the company of those who seek him, who seek the face of the God of Jacob. (Psalm 24:4, 6)

**Reflection for older children:** The gospels tell of many who sought the Lord and found him. For example, after Jesus was born, the wise men from the East saw his star and took a long journey to find him (Matthew 2:1-12). Simeon had been promised by God that he would see the Messiah before his death. Inspired by the Holy Spirit, he went to the Temple and found Mary and Joseph with the baby Jesus (Luke 2:25-38). When Jesus began his public ministry, many people sought him because they wanted to be healed.

If we seek the Lord, we will find him. We will always find the Lord at Mass in the Eucharist, where he is present—body, blood, soul, and divinity. Each week we can come to him with "clean hands and pure hearts," asking him to fill us with his love. Pray that this Christmas, you will find Christ in a special way in the Eucharist.

**Reading for younger children:** "And now your relative Elizabeth in her old age has also conceived a son; and this is the sixth month for her who was said to be barren. For nothing will be impossible with God." (Luke 1:36-37)

**Reflection for younger children:** To help Mary understand that "nothing will be impossible with God," the angel told her that Elizabeth had conceived a son when she thought she was unable to have children. There are times when things may seem "impossible" to us. So we have to keep the angel's words in mind when we are praying.

Jenny and Larry were discouraged. They had gotten married and planned to have children right away, but for three years, they were not able to have a baby. They prayed, and they asked their friends to pray as well. One evening, some friends prayed with them. These friends felt sure that the Lord was going to give Jenny and Larry a baby by the next year. Then Jenny got pregnant! The next year, her baby was born, and eventually she and Larry had six more children. They discovered that "nothing will be impossible with God."

# December 21
ZEPHANIAH 3:14-18   PSALM 33:2-3, 11-12, 20-21   LUKE 1:39-45

**Reading for older children:** When Elizabeth heard Mary's greeting, the child leaped in her womb. And Elizabeth was filled with the Holy Spirit and exclaimed with a loud cry, "Blessed are you among women, and blessed is the fruit of your womb." (Luke 1:41-42)

**Reflection for older children:** Jesus, the "fruit" of Mary's womb, was blessed. Every baby in the womb is a blessing, a cause for great joy. Human life is sacred because God is the creator of it. As Christians, we are called to do everything we can to protect human life.

One Texas builder decided to protect new life by preventing a new and expensive abortion clinic from being built in his city. When he heard about plans to build the clinic, he organized an association of contractors and tradesmen to boycott the work of building the clinic. He directed a letter-writing and telephone campaign to contact 750 businesses in his area, urging them not to provide supplies or labor for the clinic. Churches helped with calls as well. The campaign was successful, and work on the clinic stopped.

Each of us is precious in God's sight. How the Lord must celebrate every time a new child is created in the womb! Let us celebrate as well by helping others—by our words and our deeds—to understand the sanctity of life.

**Reading for younger children:** On that day it shall be said to Jerusalem: Do not fear, O Zion; do not let your hands grow weak. The LORD, your God, is in your midst, a warrior who gives victory; he will rejoice over you with gladness, he will renew you in his love; he will exult over you with loud singing. (Zephaniah 3:16-17)

**Reflection for younger children:** God does not want us to be afraid. In this reading, the prophet tells us to rejoice, for God will give us victory over our fears when we ask him.

Even adults have fears. One man suddenly became afraid to drive his car. For five years, he took the bus to work.

Then his company's office moved forty miles away. His wife volunteered to drive him for as long as he needed. The man felt so loved by his wife that he decided to do something about his fear. So he asked his wife, children, and several friends to pray for him. The first day, his wife rode in the car with him to work. Then he decided to trust God and drive alone. He has been driving ever since. God gave him a victory over his fear.

Think of a fear you have. Ask God to give you a victory over it.

# December 22

1 Samuel 1:24-28  (Psalm) 1 Samuel 2:1, 4-8  Luke 1:46-56

**Reading for older children:** And Mary said, "My soul magnifies the Lord, and my spirit rejoices in God my Savior, for he has looked with favor on the lowliness of his servant. Surely, from now on all generations will call me blessed." (Luke 1:46-48)

**Reflection for older children:** When Mary prayed this beautiful prayer, which is known as the "Magnificat," she was aware of God's great favor to her. He had chosen her to be the mother of his Son. Mary is the mother of God, but she is also our mother, because she cooperated with God's plan of salvation, which gave us new life in Christ.

As Christmas approaches, we can especially think of Mary as she and Joseph traveled to Bethlehem and searched for a place to deliver her child. In that situation, knowing that she was ready to have her baby but had no place to go, Mary may have been tempted to doubt God's care for her. And yet, God's plan was perfect.

Make time this week to pray the joyful mysteries of the rosary. As you contemplate these mysteries, think about Mary. Ask the Lord for the faith she had to trust in his plan for your life.

**Reading for younger children:** "For this child I prayed; and the LORD has granted me the petition that I made to him." (1 Samuel 1:27)

**Reflection for younger children:** Hannah was childless. She prayed to the Lord for a child, and God gave her Samuel. She was so happy that God had answered her prayer.

For years Nathan's grandparents had prayed that they would see their grandson again. When Nathan was a baby, his mother and father had divorced, and no one knew where the mother and baby had gone. Nathan's grandparents suffered a great loss without their grandson.

Several years later, after a visit with friends in Australia, the grandparents were at the airport, ready to fly home. The plane had mechanical difficulties, so while they waited, they saw a five-year-old boy who looked amazingly like their grandson Nathan. The grandfather went over to the boy, knelt down in front of him, and asked, "Is your name Nathan?" The little boy answered, "Yes."

The grandfather talked to the boy's stepfather, and sure enough, it was Nathan! The grandfather said to the grandmother, "This is not a coincidence, but a great work of God." God is so faithful. Like Hannah, he gave these grandparents the deepest desire of their hearts!

# December 23

MALACHI 3:1-4, 23-24  PSALM 25:4-5, 8-10, 14  LUKE 1:57-66

**Reading for older children:** He leads the humble in what is right, and teaches the humble his way. All the paths of the LORD are steadfast love and faithfulness, for those who keep his covenant and his decrees. (Psalm 25:9-10)

**Reflection for older children:** Jesus was born into humble circumstances. This was no accident. Our Father wanted his Son to live humbly because he wants us to be humble as well. Humble doesn't mean having a poor image of ourselves. It doesn't even mean that we are poor materially. Instead, it means not thinking we are better than others, and treating everyone with dignity and respect.

Even in competitive sports, when we are trying to win a game, we can be humble and treat the players on the opposing team the way God would want us to treat them. The coach of the Blue Thunder soccer team instructed his players to always play fairly, even if their opponents were taunting them or using illegal tactics. During one league playoff game, a player on the opposing team got angry and purposely bumped a Blue Thunder player. She fell and broke her thumb, but she tucked it under her other fingers and stayed in the game. The Blue Thunders continued to play fairly, and won the game by one goal.

**Reading for younger children:** On the eighth day they came to circumcise the child, and they were going to name him Zechariah after his father. But his mother said, "No; he is to be called John." They said to her, "None of your relatives has this name." Then they

*Fourth Week of Advent* | 85

began motioning to his father to find out what name he wanted to give him. He asked for a writing tablet and wrote, "His name is John." And all of them were amazed. (Luke 1:59-63)

**Reflection for younger children:** When you were born, your parents gave you your name. They probably thought long and hard about it, and came up with just the right name for you.

Everyone was surprised that Zechariah and Elizabeth had not chosen "Zechariah" for their son's name, because it was common practice for fathers to name their sons after them. But God had come up with just the right name for their son. John means "God is gracious." God was gracious to Zechariah and Elizabeth, because after so many years of being childless, he had given them a son. God was also gracious to us, because John had a special role to play in God's kingdom. He would be the "herald," announcing the coming of the Messiah, Jesus.

The Bible tells us that God calls each one of us by name (Isaiah 43:1). He promises never to forget us. In fact, God says our names are inscribed on the palms of his hands (49:16)! And like John, God has a special role for each of us to play in building his kingdom on earth. Think about one special thing you can do today to help build God's kingdom in your family.

# December 24 (Readings for Morning Mass)
2 Samuel 7:1-5, 8-12, 14, 16   Psalm 89:2-5, 27, 29   Luke 1:67-79

**Reading for older children:** You said, "I have made a covenant with my chosen one, I have sworn to my servant David: 'I will establish your descendants forever, and build your throne for all generations.' " (Psalm 89:3-4)

**Reflection for older children:** Long ago, one thousand years before the birth of Jesus, God made a promise to King David. Through the prophet Nathan, the Lord told him: "Your house and your kingdom shall be made sure forever before me; your throne shall be established forever" (2 Samuel 7:16).

As a descendent of David, Jesus is the fulfillment of that promise. The church uses this reading on the day before Christmas to remind us of what God had planned since the beginning. David was an earthly king, but Jesus is an eternal king. His kingdom will last forever.

This evening or tomorrow, you will celebrate Christmas by exchanging gifts with your family and friends. Like the wise men, come to the crèche with gifts for the newborn king. Rather than gifts of gold, frankincense, and myrrh, however, you can give Jesus the gift of your heart. It's the gift he most desires, because when we give him our hearts, he fills it with his love.

**Reading for younger children:** "And you, child, will be called the prophet of the Most High; for you will go before the Lord to prepare his ways, to give knowledge of salvation to his people by the forgiveness of their sins." (Luke 1:76-77)

**Reflection for younger children:** As a father waited in line in the store to pay for his Christmas gifts, he listened to the impatient and anxious comments of the other shoppers. Somehow he wanted to remind everyone that Christmas was about celebrating the birth of Jesus. On his way home, he had an idea.

The following day, the father hired a donkey, dressed his daughter as Mary and his son as Joseph. He dressed himself as a shepherd. He lifted Mary onto the donkey, gave Joseph a staff and the donkey's reins, and led them carefully along the streets of the city.

People waved from their cars and honked their horns. Others called out, "Thank you!" There were articles with photographs in several newspapers. A local television station highlighted their journey. Just as John the Baptist prepared the way for Christ two thousand years ago, this father and his children prepared the way for the Lord in their city that year.

# 4

## Special Feast Days

# Feast of St. Andrew (November 30)

ROMANS 10:9-18   PSALM 19:8-11   MATTHEW 4:18-22

**Reading for older children:** But how are they to call on one in whom they have not believed? And how are they to believe in one of whom they have never heard? And how are they to hear without someone to proclaim him? And how are they to proclaim him unless they are sent? (Romans 10:14-15)

**Reflection for older children:** St. Andrew had been a fisherman and disciple of John the Baptist before he became a follower of Jesus and one of the twelve apostles. After Jesus' resurrection, Andrew was "sent" to proclaim the gospel in southern Russia and Byzantium. By the time he was martyred, many people had come to believe in Jesus.

In a book called *Bruchko*, Bruce Olson relates how, when he was nineteen years old, he was sent by God to proclaim the gospel to the Colombian Motilone tribe. Members of the tribe had never allowed outsiders to visit them and knew nothing about Christ. When Olson walked into the jungle, he was shot through the leg with a five-foot-long spear and held captive for months, all the while expecting to be executed.

But Bruce never doubted God was with him, for the Lord had given him a great love and compassion for these people. After observing his life and hearing him speak about Jesus, everyone in the entire Motilone tribe became Christian. He lived among them for twenty-eight years, proclaiming Jesus in word and action.

**Reading for younger children:** As [Jesus] walked by the Sea of Galilee, he saw two brothers, Simon, who is called Peter, and

Andrew his brother, casting a net into the sea—for they were fishermen. And he said to them, "Follow me, and I will make you fish for people." Immediately they left their nets and followed him. (Matthew 4:18-20)

**Reflection for younger children:** Sometimes following Jesus is difficult. One boy named Michael complained, "I don't want Roger to come over anymore. He always wants to play indoor games and computer games, but he's so slow. I want to wrestle, ride bikes, and play football."

Michael's father said to him, "Sometimes following Jesus means giving up what you want to do. Remember what Jesus' friends did? Peter and Andrew gave up fishing to follow Jesus. When you were baptized, Christ came to live in you. When you play what Roger wants, you allow Christ in you to love your friend."

"That's going to be hard," Michael said.

But the next time Roger came to play, Michael let him play computer games and didn't touch the keys when he was too slow. He told his dad later, "It was hard, but I did it."

# Feast of the Immaculate Conception of the Blessed Virgin Mary (December 8)
### GENESIS 3:9-15, 20    PSALM 98:1-4
### EPHESIANS 1:3-6, 11-12    LUKE 1:26-38

**Reading for older children:** He chose us in Christ before the foundation of the world to be holy and blameless before him in love. (Ephesians 1:4)

**Reflection for older children:** "I am the Immaculate Conception." The Blessed Virgin Mary said these words to St. Bernadette Soubirous in 1858 in Lourdes, France. Bernadette, who was only fourteen and illiterate, had no idea what the words meant. But all the way back from the grotto, where she had seen apparitions of Mary, she repeated them. Three years earlier, Pope Pius IX had defined the term to mean that Mary was, from the first instant of her conception, preserved from original sin.

In a special way, Mary was chosen "to be holy and blameless" before God. She was to be the perfect vessel for God's Son. Mary is our mother, and she calls us to holiness by leading us to her Son Jesus. Because of Mary's appearances at Lourdes, many people began to follow Jesus. Even today, many people are healed and their faith strengthened as they travel to Lourdes and bathe in the water from a spring that miraculously began to flow there while Mary was appearing to Bernadette.

**Reading for younger children:** Mary said, "Here am I, the servant of the Lord; let it be with me according to your word" (Luke 1:38).

**Reflection for younger children:** Before Mary was born, our Father planned for her to be the mother of Jesus. From the moment she came into being, he kept her pure and without sin. Mary loved and served God from the time she was a young child. She called herself the servant of the Lord.

So when the angel Gabriel asked her to be the mother of Jesus, Mary was ready to say yes. She wanted to do whatever God asked her to do. She wanted to follow his plan for her life.

How can you be a servant of the Lord? Jesus is pleased even with the simplest service—like doing a chore your parents ask of you or watching your little brother or sister when your mom or dad is busy. Blessed Mother Teresa of Calcutta used to say that we can do even little things with great love. The love we have as we serve is as important as the service itself!

## Feast of Our Lady of Guadalupe (December 12)
### ZECHARIAH 2:14-17  PSALM 145:1, 9-13
### ROMANS 8:28-30  LUKE 2:15-19

**Reading for older and younger children:** When the angels had left them and gone into heaven, the shepherds said to one another, "Let us go now to Bethlehem and see this thing that has taken place, which the Lord has made known to us." (Luke 2:15)

**Reflection for older and younger children:** Juan Diego was simple and humble like the shepherds. He was a poor, middle-aged Aztec Indian who became a convert when Spain ruled Mexico. He had to walk many miles to Mass.

On his way to Mass on December 9, 1531, Juan saw a brilliant light and heard beautiful music up on the hill of Tepeyac. He followed the music and at the top, in the midst of the light, stood the Virgin Mary, her face as dark as his own. She spoke to Juan in his native Aztec language. She asked him to tell the bishop to build a shrine on this hill. Here she would show her love, compassion, and protection to the people.

After waiting for hours, Juan told the bishop about Mary's wishes. But the bishop called them pious daydreams. Juan went back and told Mary that he had failed, and begged her to send a more noteworthy person to the bishop, since he was only a poor peasant. She told him to go again the next day.

The next day, the bishop asked for a sign. He wanted Juan to bring roses that grow only in Spain. Juan told Our Lady, and she promised to grant his request the following morning.

But the following morning, Juan's uncle was dying, and Juan had to go for a priest. On the way, Our Lady appeared. She asked Juan why he had not come to her. Our Lady said, "Let not your heart be disturbed. Be assured—he is already well." Then she told him to pick the roses.

Juan knew the hill was nothing but sand, rock, and cactus. Besides, it was not the season for roses. But when Juan reached the top, roses were everywhere. Juan gathered them into his tilma—a hooded cloak—and rushed to the bishop.

As Juan opened his tilma, the flowers fell to the floor. To the bishop's astonishment, imprinted on Juan's coarse tilma was the image of Our Lady of Guadalupe—which, translated from the Aztec language, means she who crushes the serpent.

To this day Juan Diego's tilma hangs in the church built on the hill in Our Lady of Guadalupe's honor. More than twenty-two languages were spoken at that time, but everyone could understand the sacred image of Our Lady. Within seven years, eight million natives were converted to Christianity.

# 5

# The Jesse Tree

The Jesse Tree is a hands-on activity that helps children to understand the history of our redemption, from creation to the birth of Jesus. Jesus came from the house or line of King David. King David was the son of Jesse. The prophet Isaiah was speaking of Jesus when he foretold that a shoot would spring from the root of Jesse (Isaiah 11:1, 10). Each day for twenty-nine days, children hear a story about a key biblical figure who preceded Jesus. Before or after the prayer, children can make a symbol for the story, such as an ark for Noah or a hammer for St. Joseph, and place it on a tree. By the time Christmas arrives, the tree is fully decorated.

The Jesse Tree readings can be said at morning prayer or after lighting the Advent wreath. You may want to read the Scripture cited—perhaps from a children's Bible—or a parent could tell the story after reading the Scripture ahead of time. Another option is to read the scriptural synopsis provided here.

The responses to the story may be used as a litany, adding each day's response to those of the previous days. As it takes longer and longer to recite, a child will experience how long the world waited for Jesus. At the same time, the child's eager expectation increases as the time before Christmas grows shorter.

After reading the story and litany, have your children hang the symbol of that story on a tree. You may create your own symbols or use the ones suggested. Hang the symbol from a bare branch placed in a planter or pail of dirt or on an undecorated evergreen tree. Or, you may want to make a felt evergreen tree and symbols to keep from year to year.

# Readings for the Jesse Tree
## Day 1
### CREATION: GENESIS 1; 2:3

In the beginning, before God created the heavens and earth, darkness was everywhere. Then a mighty wind from God swept over the earth, and God said, "Let there be light." And there was light. God separated light from darkness and called it Day and Night. He created earth and water, every kind of plant, and every kind of animal and bird. Then he created humankind, male and female. He created them in his image and likeness.

And on the seventh day, God rested and saw that everything he created was good.

**Litany Reader:** When God made the world, he was already planning to send his Son into a world that waited for the Savior.

**Response:** We are waiting too, O Lord.

**Symbol:** Globe of the world

## Day 2
### PROMISES TO ADAM AND EVE: GENESIS 2:15-17; 3:1-24

God put Adam and Eve in the Garden of Eden and told them to take care of it. He told them they could eat the fruit of every tree except the tree of the knowledge of good and evil. He said if they ate the fruit from this tree, they would die.

But a serpent lied to Eve. He said they wouldn't die; instead they would be like God. So Eve ate the fruit and gave some to her husband. Then they knew they were naked and covered themselves with fig leafs.

When Adam and Eve heard God coming, they hid. But God found them. He asked Adam why he ate the fruit and who told him he was naked. Adam said Eve gave it to him, and Eve said the serpent tricked her. God told the serpent he would always have to crawl on his belly.

Because Adam and Eve disobeyed God, they had to leave the garden and they would have to die someday. God placed the cherubim and a flaming sword to guard the way to the tree of life.

**Litany Reader:** Adam and Eve disobeyed God; then they waited for the Savior.

**Response:** We are waiting too, O Lord.

**Symbol:** Apple

# Day 3
## CAIN AND ABEL: GENESIS 4:1-16

Adam and Eve had two sons, Cain and Abel. Cain was a farmer and Abel was a shepherd. Cain offered God his fruits and vegetables and Abel gave God his firstborn lambs. God accepted Abel's offering. But did not accept Cain's offering, and Cain became angry. God told Cain he would accept his offering if he did well. God also warned him to master his sin. Cain's anger turned to jealousy of his brother. So Cain killed Abel.

The Lord asked Cain, "Where is your brother?"

Cain answered, "Am I my brother's keeper?"

God said, "Because you have killed him, your fields will no longer bear abundant produce, and you will be a wanderer on the earth forever."

God put a mark on Cain so no one would kill him. Then Cain went away from the presence of the Lord.

**Litany Reader:** Abel was killed by his brother while he waited for the Savior.

**Response:** We are waiting too, O Lord.

**Symbol:** Knife

# Day 4
### NOAH: GENESIS 6:5-14, 22; 7:17, 23–8:1, 20-22; 9:8-17

Humans became violent, so God planned to send a great flood to destroy all living things on the earth. But because Noah and his family were righteous, God told Noah to build an ark and to take two of every living thing with him into the ark. Noah and his family did all that God commanded.

God sent rain for forty days and forty nights. After the waters retreated, the ark rested on the mountain of Ararat. God made a covenant with them. He promised he would never destroy every living creature again. As a sign of his promise, God set a rainbow in the sky.

**Litany Reader:** Noah floated in the ark, waiting for the Savior.

**Response:** We are waiting too, O Lord.

**Symbol:** Ark

# Day 5
## ABRAHAM: GENESIS 12:1-7; 17:1-22

Abram was a descendant of Noah. Abram was seventy-five years old when the Lord told him to leave his land with his wife, all his people and possessions, and go to a land the Lord would show him. And Abram did what the Lord told him.

When Abram was ninety-nine years old and his wife Sarai was ninety, God told Abram his offspring would inherit the land. Abram and Sarai were childless, so Abram laughed to think that an old man and woman could have a child. But God told Abram that kings would come from Sarai. Sarai would have a son, Isaac, and God would establish his covenant with Isaac and his offspring after him. God changed Abram's name to Abraham and Sarai's name to Sarah.

**Litany Reader:** Abraham walked to the Promised Land, waiting for the Savior.

**Response:** We are waiting too, O Lord.

**Symbol:** Walking stick

# Day 6
## ISAAC: GENESIS 22:1-18

One day God wanted to test Abraham's love and faithfulness. He told Abraham to go to a mountain, build an altar and sacrifice his son, Isaac, as a burnt offering to him. So Abraham put some wood on Isaac's back. Abraham carried the fire and knife, and they set out.

Isaac asked, "We have the wood, the knife, and the fire, but where is the lamb for the burnt offering?"

Abraham answered, "God will provide the burnt offering, my son."

When they reached the mountain, Abraham built an altar, laid wood on it, tied up his son, and laid him on the altar. Then he took the knife to kill him. But an angel of the Lord called from heaven, saying, "Abraham, do not lay your hand on your son, for now I know you love me since you have not withheld your only son from me."

Abraham looked up and saw a ram caught in a thicket by its horns, and he offered it up as a burnt offering instead of his son. The Lord said, "Because you have not withheld your only son, I will bless you. Your descendants will be as numerous as the stars of heaven and as the sand on the seashore."

**Litany Reader:** Abraham was willing to give up his only son while he waited for the Savior.

**Response:** We are waiting too, O Lord.

**Symbol:** A small bundle of sticks

# Day 7

## JACOB (ISRAEL): GENESIS 28:1-17

When Isaac grew up, he had two sons. One of his sons was called Jacob. Isaac told Jacob to journey to the land where his mother's people lived to find a wife. So Jacob left his country and set out. One night as he was sleeping, he dreamed there was a ladder reaching from earth to heaven and that the angels of God were going up and down on it. The Lord stood beside Jacob and said, "I am the LORD, the God of Abraham and Isaac; the land on which you lie I will give to you and your offspring. And your offspring shall be like the dust of the earth spreading from west to east and north to south; and all families of the earth will be blessed in you and in your offspring. I will watch over you wherever you go and bring you back to this land."

Then Jacob awoke and said, "Surely the LORD is in this place—and I did not know it! How awesome is this place! This is none other than the house of God, and this is the gate of heaven."

**Litany Reader:** Jacob saw a ladder reaching up to heaven while he waited for the Savior.

**Response:** We are waiting too, O Lord.

**Symbol:** A ladder

# Day 8
## Joseph: Genesis 37:1-4, 28; 39:1-5; 41:46-57; 42:1-6, 43-44; 45:1-15

Jacob had twelve sons. (These became the twelve tribes of Israel.) He loved Joseph, the youngest, more than the rest and made him a coat of many colors. The other brothers were jealous of Joseph, and when they were out with their flocks they sold Joseph to some traders. Joseph became the slave to one of the officials of the Egyptian Pharaoh.

Then when he was thirty years old, Joseph became the steward of Pharaoh, king of Egypt. Joseph told Pharaoh there would be seven years of plenty in the land followed by seven years of famine. So Joseph had grain saved in the years of plenty, and during the famine the whole world came to him for grain.

His brothers came as well, but they did not recognize Joseph. Joseph told them who he was and said they should not be distressed that they had sold him, because it was God's plan to bring them all to Egypt. The Pharaoh had told Joseph to bring his brothers and their wives and children, his aged father Jacob, and all their possessions to Egypt. And the twelve sons of Israel, as Jacob was called, left the land of Canaan and dwelt in Egypt.

**Litany Reader:** Joseph was sold into slavery in Egypt, where he waited for the Savior.

**Response:** We are waiting too, O Lord.

**Symbol:** Coat of many colors

# Day 9
### JUDAH: GENESIS 49:1, 8-10

When Jacob was dying, he called his sons to him and said: "Gather around your father, Israel, that I may tell you what will happen to you in the days to come."

When he laid his hand on his son Judah, he said, "Judah, your brothers shall praise you. You will be like a lion and defeat your enemies. Your descendants will rule, and people will be obedient to you."

**Litany Reader:** God told Judah his descendant would be king. Judah waited for the Savior.

**Response:** We are waiting too, O Lord.

**Symbol:** Lion with a crown on its head (One of the names for Jesus is the Lion of Judah.)

# Day 10
### MOSES: EXODUS 1:8–3:12

A new king arose in Egypt who did not know Joseph. He decided to make the people of Israel work hard because they were more numerous than the Egyptians. He also had all the boy babies of the Israelites—or Hebrews as they were also called—thrown in the Nile River. But Moses was saved by Pharaoh's daughter and was raised by her in the palace.

When Moses grew up, he found out he was a Hebrew. He saw an Egyptian flogging a Hebrew and killed him, then fled from Egypt to Midian. He married and lived as a shepherd. One day as he watched his sheep, he saw a bush on fire but it did not burn up, so he went to investigate.

God called out to him from the burning bush, "Moses, Moses!" Moses answered, "Here I am."

God told Moses to take off his shoes, for he was standing on holy ground. Moses took off his shoes. Then God said, "I am the God of your father, the God of Abraham, the God of Isaac, and the God of Jacob. I see that my people are in misery, and I have heard their cry for deliverance. So I will send you to Pharaoh to bring my people, the Israelites, out of Egypt."

**Litany Reader:** God showed himself to Moses in the burning bush and sent him to lead his people out of slavery. Moses waited for the Savior.

**Response:** We are waiting too, O Lord.

**Symbol:** Burning bush

# Day 11
## THE TEN COMMANDMENTS: DEUTERONOMY 30:15-20

Moses talked with Pharaoh many times, and God sent plagues on the Egyptians. Finally Pharaoh let the Hebrews leave Egypt. But while they were on their way to the Promised Land, they began to complain against God, treat one another badly, and worship false gods. So God had them wander around in the desert for forty years.

Then God told Moses to have the people wait while he talked with him on a mountain. The Lord gave Moses commandments for the people to live by. So Moses told the people that the Lord said, "I have set before you life and death. Choose life so that you and your descendants may live, loving the Lord your God, obeying him, and holding fast to him, so that you may live in the land that I gave to your ancestors, Abraham, Isaac, and Jacob."

**Litany Reader:** God gave Moses the Law, but it could not free the people from their sins. They waited for the Savior.

**Response:** We are waiting too, O Lord.

**Symbol:** The Tablet of the Ten Commandments

# Day 12
## JOSHUA: JOSHUA 1:1-2; 6:8-16, 20

After Moses died, God chose Joshua, Moses' assistant, to lead his people. So Joshua led his people across the Jordan, but when they reached Jericho the gates were shut up against them. Then God said to Joshua, "I have handed Jericho over to you. March around the city once for six days, blaring the trumpets before the Ark of the Covenant. On the seventh day, march around the city seven times, and when the trumpets blare, have the people raise a great shout." Joshua did what the Lord commanded, and the walls of Jericho fell down.

**Litany Reader:** When Joshua marched around Jericho, the walls fell down. He waited for the Savior.

**Response:** We are waiting too, O Lord.

**Symbol:** Trumpet

# Day 13
### RUTH: RUTH 1:1-9, 14-19; 2:1-4; 4:13, 17

In the days when judges ruled Israel, there was a famine in the land. So Elimelech, a man from Bethlehem in Judah, along with his wife Naomi and their two sons, went to live in Moab. Both sons married Moabite women. One son married a woman named Ruth.

After a time Elimelech and his sons died, and Naomi decided to return to the land of Judah. One daughter-in-law went back to her people, but Ruth said to Naomi, "I am going with you. Your people shall be my people, and your God my God." So Naomi and Ruth journeyed back to Bethlehem.

It was barley harvest time, and Naomi told Ruth to gather grain left behind by the reapers in Boaz's field. Boaz was Elimelech's relative, and he would take care of her. Soon Ruth and Boaz married and had a son named Obed. Obed became the father of Jesse. Jesse became the father of King David.

**Litany Reader:** Ruth was faithful to her mother-in-law and so she became the great-grandmother of David, while she waited for the Savior.

**Response:** We are waiting too, O Lord.

**Symbol:** Sheaf of grain

# Day 14
## SAMUEL: 1 SAMUEL 3:1-11, 19-21

Young Samuel was serving God with Eli, the priest. While Samuel was lying in the sanctuary before the Ark of the Covenant, he heard a call: "Samuel! Samuel!" Samuel ran to Eli and answered, "Here I am!" But Eli said, "I did not call you." When this happened a second and third time, Eli said, "Go and lie down, and when you hear the call, answer, 'Speak, LORD, for your servant is listening.'"

So Samuel answered Yahweh's call, saying, "Speak, LORD, for your servant is listening."

The Lord said, "I am going to do something in Israel which will make the ears of all who hear of it ring."

When Samuel grew up, the Lord was with him, and all Israel knew that Samuel was a trustworthy prophet of the Lord.

**Litany Reader:** The word of God came to the prophet Samuel, for he waited for the Savior.

**Response:** We are waiting too, O Lord.

**Symbol:** An ear or a footprint with the words, "Speak, for your servant is listening."

# Day 15

The Lord told Samuel to go to Jesse in Bethlehem, for there was a king among his sons. Jesse brought seven sons before Samuel, but when Samuel looked into their hearts, he knew none of them was to be king.

Samuel asked Jesse if he had any other sons. Jesse had his youngest son, David, brought from the fields, where he was keeping sheep. When David came in, the Lord said to Samuel, "Anoint him, for this one shall be king."

**Litany Reader:** Jesse was a shepherd whose son became king as he waited for the Savior.

**Response:** We are waiting too, O Lord.

**Symbol:** Roots of a tree, since Jesus is called "The Root of Jesse"

# Day 16

**DAVID:** 2 SAMUEL 7:1-2, 4-5, 12-17

When David became king, he said, "I am living in a house of cedar while the Ark of God stays in a tent. I will build a house for God." But the prophet Nathan told King David that the Lord said, "One of your offspring shall build a house for my name, and I will establish the throne of his kingdom forever. I will be a father to him, and he will be a son to me. I will not take my steadfast love from him. Your house and your kingdom shall be made sure forever."

**Litany Reader:** God promised David he would always have a son on the throne. David waited for the Savior.

**Response:** We are waiting too, O Lord.

**Symbol:** King's crown

# Day 17
## Solomon: 1 Kings 8:14-15, 20-24

When King David died, his son Solomon became king. He built a temple for God and said, "Blessed be the LORD, the God of Israel who with his hand has fulfilled what he promised to my father David, that I would sit on the throne of my father and build a house for the name of the LORD, the God of Israel."

**Litany Reader:** Solomon, the wisest man who ever lived, built a glorious temple for the Lord, and he waited for the Savior.

**Response:** We are waiting too, O Lord.

**Symbol:** Temple

# Day 18
## ELIJAH: 1 KINGS 18:17-39

Elijah was a true prophet of the Lord. But the ruler Ahab liked what the false prophets told him—that he and the people should worship the false god Baal. So Ahab planned to kill Elijah because he prophesied the truth that the Lord was God.

Elijah had a plan to show Ahab and the people that the Lord was God and not the false god Baal. He had two bulls brought, one for him and one for the false prophets. He had them cut in pieces and laid on wood. He told the false prophets to pray to their god, but he would pray to the Lord God of Israel. Whichever God sent fire from heaven to consume their bull would be the true God.

So the false prophets prayed all day, but Baal sent no fire to consume their bull.

Elijah had water poured three times on his bull and on the wood. He prayed, "O LORD, God of Abraham, Isaac, and Israel, let it be known this day that you are God in Israel, that I am your servant, and that I have done all these things at your bidding. Turn the hearts of your people back to you."

Then fire came from heaven and consumed Elijah's bull. When all the people saw it, they fell on their faces and said, "The LORD is indeed God!"

**Litany Reader:** Fire came down from heaven when the prophet Elijah prayed, and he waited for the Savior.

**Response:** We are waiting too, O Lord.

**Symbol:** Fire

# Day 19
## Isaiah: Isaiah 6:1-8; 7:14

Isaiah saw a vision of angels and heard them call to one another: "Holy, holy, holy is the LORD of hosts; the whole earth is full of his glory." The house shook and began to fill with clouds of smoke. Isaiah said, "I have seen the King, the Lord of Hosts; I, a man of unclean lips who dwells among a people of unclean lips."

Then one of the angels touched Isaiah's lips with a burning coal, saying, "Now that this has touched your lips, your guilt has departed and your sin is blotted out."

Isaiah heard the voice of the Lord say, "Whom shall I send, and who will go for us?"

Isaiah said, "Here am I; send me!"

So Isaiah became a prophet of the Lord and prophesied to the people that the Lord God would give them a sign: a virgin would give birth to a son and call him Immanuel.

**Litany Reader:** The prophet Isaiah told us the Messiah would be born of a virgin. He waited for the Savior.

**Response:** We are waiting too, O Lord.

**Symbol:** An angel with a burning coal

# Day 20
## MICAH: MICAH 5:2

Other prophets told about a Savior coming. The prophet Micah said, "But you, O Bethlehem of Ephrathah, too small to be among the clans of Judah, from you shall come forth for me one who is to rule in Israel, whose origin is from of old, from ancient days."

**Litany Reader:** The prophet Micah told us the Messiah would be born in Bethlehem. He waited for the Savior.

**Response:** We are waiting too, O Lord.

**Symbol:** A star over a manger

# Day 21
## JEREMIAH: JEREMIAH 23:1-6; 38:3-6

Jeremiah was a prophet, too. He told the rulers of Judah that they were like shepherds that destroy and scatter their sheep. He said that God would raise up for David a righteous branch—a king who would deal wisely and do what is right and just. He also told the rulers other things that they didn't like to hear, so they threw him in an empty well, and Jeremiah sank in the mud to the bottom.

**Litany Reader:** Jeremiah suffered for proclaiming God's judgment on Judah. He waited for the Savior.

**Response:** We are waiting too, O Lord.

**Symbol:** A well

# Day 22
## DANIEL: DANIEL 1:1-6; 2:44-49; 6:11-28

God's people were taken from their country and sent into exile in Babylon. Daniel was one of the exiles. He was a prophet who could tell the meaning of dreams. Daniel said that God would set up a kingdom that would never be destroyed.

One Babylonian king knew God was with Daniel, so he planned to make Daniel ruler over his kingdom. But other men wanted to rule, so they told lies about Daniel and tricked the king into punishing him by throwing him into a lions' den.

The king loved Daniel and told him to pray to his God for protection.   Daniel prayed, and the lions didn't harm him. The king decreed that the whole world should worship Daniel's God, the living God.

**Litany Reader:** Daniel was delivered from lions to speak God's message as he waited for the Savior.

**Response:** We are waiting too, O Lord.

**Symbol:** Lion

# Day 23

**EZEKIEL:** EZEKIEL 37:21-28

The prophet Ezekiel told the Israelites that they would no longer live among other nations. They would live in their own land and have one ruler. This ruler would be like a kind shepherd. Ezekiel said God would live with the Israelites forever. He would be their God, and they would be his people.

**Litany Reader:** Ezekiel told the people God would lead them back to their land. They waited for a Savior.

**Response:** We are waiting too, O Lord.

**Symbol:** A shepherd

# Day 24

**MALACHI:** MALACHI 3:1-3; 4:1-2

Malachi is the last prophet of the Old Testament. He said God was sending a messenger in whom the people of Israel would delight. But first they needed to prepare for him by purifying their proud hearts. Then to those who love him, "the sun of righteousness shall rise with healing in its wings."

**Litany Reader:** The prophet Malachi promised that the Savior would come like the sun. At the end of the Old Testament, Israel still waited for the Savior.

**Response:** We are waiting too, O Lord.

**Symbol:** Sun

# Day 25
## ZECHARIAH: LUKE 1:5-22

A priest named Zechariah was offering incense in the sanctuary of the Lord when an angel appeared to him. The angel told him that his wife, Elizabeth, would have a son. The angel said that they should name him John. And even before he was born, John would be filled with the Holy Spirit. The angel said that many would rejoice in John. He would turn many hearts to the Lord and help the people prepare for the Lord's coming.

Zechariah doubted he could have a son because he and his wife were old. Because he doubted the angel's words, he was unable to speak until his son, John, was born.

**Litany Reader:** God told Zechariah he would have a son in his old age.  He waited for the Savior.

**Response:** We are waiting too, O Lord.

**Symbol:** Smoke rising from an incense burner

# Day 26

**JOHN THE BAPTIST:** MATTHEW 3:1-6; JOHN 1:29-31

When John grew up, he lived in the wilderness. He wore clothing of camel's hair and ate wild locusts and honey. People came from Jerusalem and Judea so he could baptize them in the Jordan River. These people repented of their sins to get ready for the Savior.

One day John baptized Jesus and saw the Holy Spirit rest on him. He told everyone that Jesus was the Lamb of God who takes away the sins of the world. He told them Jesus was the Son of God, the Savior they had been waiting for.

**Litany Reader:** John cried out in the desert, "God's kingdom is about to come!" He pointed to the Lamb of God because he and all of Israel waited for the Savior.

**Response:** We are waiting too, O Lord.

**Symbol:** Pot of honey

# Day 27

**JOSEPH:** MATTHEW 1:18-25

Joseph, of the House of David, was a carpenter who was engaged to Mary. But before they were married he discovered she was with child. An angel appeared to Joseph in a dream and told him not to be afraid to take Mary as his wife. The baby within her was conceived by the Holy Spirit. The angel said that the baby would be a son and that he should be named Jesus, for he would save his people from their sins.

**Litany Reader:** Joseph worked with a hammer. He saw an angel while he waited for the Savior.

**Response:** We are waiting too, O Lord.

**Symbol:** Hammer or saw

# Day 28
## MARY: LUKE 1:26-38

The angel Gabriel visited Mary, saying, "Greetings, favored one! The Lord is with you."

Mary was afraid. She didn't understand why an angel would greet her like this.

But Gabriel told her not to be afraid, because she would bear a son who would be great. The Lord God would give her son the throne of his ancestor David, and his kingdom would have no end. He told her the Holy Spirit would come upon her and the child would be the Son of God. Then the angel told her about Zechariah and Elizabeth having a baby in their old age. The angel said, "Nothing will be impossible with God."

Mary said, "I am the servant of the Lord. Let it be done unto me according to your word."

**Litany Reader:** The angel Gabriel told Mary she would be the virgin mother of the Messiah. Then Mary waited for the birth of the Savior.

**Response:** We are waiting too, O Lord.

**Symbol:** Holy Spirit in the form of a dove

# Day 29
## JESUS: LUKE 2:1-20

The Emperor Augustus wanted to know how many people there were in the world, so he had every family register in their native town. Because Joseph was from the family of David, he and Mary traveled from Nazareth to Bethlehem, the city of David. But the city was crowded, and they couldn't find a place to stay. Joseph found a clean, warm place where animals were kept. Soon Jesus was born there. Mary wrapped Jesus in bands of cloth and laid him in a manger.

**Litany Reader:** Jesus, you are the Savior we have been waiting for.

**Response:** We welcome you, O Lord.

**Symbol:** A baby in a manger, a crown of thorns, or a cross

# 6

## Advent Angels and the Christ Child Crib
## The Little Juggler

# Advent Angels and the Christ Child Crib

In her book *Mother Teresa*, Kathryn Spink writes:

> In preparation for Christmas, the season when the 'Word was made flesh and dwelt among us,' an empty crib would be placed in the Sisters' chapel. Also in the chapel was a box containing some straw. During advent, the Sisters were encouraged to make small personal sacrifices, to allow someone else readier access to the water tank, for example, by relinquishing their own place. Then, discreetly, they would go to the chapel, remove a straw from the box and place it in the crib. Thus when the infant Jesus was laid in the manger at Christmas it would be in a crib warmed by their love and sacrifice. (*Mother Teresa: A Complete Authorized Biography*, HarperCollins Publishers, Inc., 1998)

Children love secrets and surprises. So it's no wonder many families have adopted the Advent Angel/Christ Child Crib tradition. On the first Sunday of Advent, a "crib" is placed in a readily accessible place in the house, with a box of "straw" next to it. Family members may choose to be an Advent "angel" to everyone in the family throughout Advent, or they may draw names weekly or keep the same name the entire four weeks. Delightful squeals accompany the revealing of Advent angels at the end of each week or at the end of Advent.

After the Advent angel secretly performs a kindness, which may be as simple as doing a chore or placing a note in a shoe, then the angel—also secretly—places a straw in the Christ Child's crib. A parent may have to whisper ideas for a kindness to little ones and remind them to put a "straw" in the crib.

The crib can be made from a box or wood. One family had a porcelain crib (and babe) they placed in the middle of their dining room table. If no straw is available, narrow strips of yellow construction or crepe paper can be used. For years our crib consisted of half an oatmeal box, and the Christ Child was a doll wrapped in white cloth. Then a generous uncle made us a wooden cradle.

This tradition, with its heightened awareness of serving others, is often carried over to other seasons of the year and passed on to future generations. Sons and daughters have incorporated the tradition into their families' Advent celebrations. One college student introduced her dorm mates to the tradition. It made them more aware of serving one another. Christ's love grows in hearts looking for opportunities to be kind.

# The Little Juggler of Notre Dame

When I was a young mother, during Advent—when zeal as Advent angels waned—we read or acted out the story of *The Little Juggler*. His desire to give a special gift to the Christ child and his mother cheered us on to loving service.

Our children loved puppet shows, so they drew the characters on paper, colored them, cut them out, and glued them to ice pop sticks. The puppeteers hid behind a couch, then popped up on cue whenever their character appeared in the story. There are several versions of this story, but the paraphrased one below is from Barbara Cooney's book *The Little Juggler* (Hastings House, 1986). It is based on an old French legend known as "The Juggler of Notre Dame."

Without parents or relatives, the little juggler was earning his living at ten years old the only way he knew how—by juggling and tumbling. In market squares, at fairs, weddings, and sometimes in castles, he rolled out the shabby rug that carried his hoops, balls, and sticks, and juggled, tumbled, sang, and danced. When the weather was warm, he earned his bread, but then winter came. The markets were empty, there were no fairs, and the bridges were up at the castles.

One day he was almost frozen in spite of his juggling and tumbling, and the only person at the market was a monk from the nearby abbey.

The monk asked the boy where he lived, and upon hearing he had no home, the monk took him to live in the abbey.

The little juggler was happy to have warm clothes, food, and a place to sleep. But one day as he walked through the abbey, he saw how all the monks served God at their assigned tasks. He thought: "I should not be here. I have nothing I can do for God." He was sadder yet when, during Advent, he saw the monks working on gifts to present to the Christ child and his mother on Christmas Eve. One was composing a song, another a poem. Several copied books in beautiful writing and others worked together carving a statue.

One day the little juggler knelt before a statue of the Blessed Mother and asked, "Holy Mother, how can I serve you? I have nothing to give to you and your child." Then he wept and wept. But as the bells for Mass rang, he got an idea. "Dear Lady," he said, "The only thing I have to give is my tumbling and juggling. With God's help I will do it with all my heart."

Every day while the monks were at Mass, the little juggler removed his robe, rolled out his shabby rug, and juggled and tumbled with all his heart before the Christ child and his mother.

But one of the monks had noticed that the little juggler missed Mass every day, and two days before Christmas he followed him and watched from behind a pillar. He thought: "I think the sins of us all together cannot equal this. I must tell the abbot."

On Christmas Eve, the little juggler watched all the monks present their beautiful gifts to the Christ child and his mother. Then after they returned to their cells, the little juggler crept back to the altar. The abbot and monk watched from behind a pillar.

"Blessed Mother, I cannot match the splendor of their gifts, but I will give you the only thing I have to give." Then he tumbled and juggled with all his might until exhausted, he sank to the ground and fell asleep.

Suddenly, the abbot and spying monk saw Our Lady, surrounded by angels, walk down from the statue's niche to where the little juggler slept. She wiped his brow, kissed him, and returned to her niche.

The spying monk, filled with shame, said, "Surely I have judged him wrongly."

The day after Christmas the abbot sent for the little juggler. Trembling with fear, he knelt before the abbot. "I have done nothing to earn my bread and know I should be sent away."

The abbot raised the little juggler from his knees and said, "Little brother, I promise you may stay here always and do this service— just as you have before—and as well as you know how."

So every day, with all his heart, the little juggler plied his craft before the Christ child and his mother.

# About the Author

Julie Walters is a freelance writer and the author of several children's books. Her most recent books include *St. Elizabeth Ann Seton: Saint for a New Nation* (Paulist Press, 2002) and *God Is Like* (Waterbrook Press, 2000). *The Secrets of the Twelve Days of Christmas* will be published by Paulist Press next year. She has written articles for *Catholic Digest, Liguorian Magazine,* and *Our Daily Visitor.* She has also written a preschool manual using Montessori teaching methods. Julie and her husband Clem have four children and eleven grandchildren and reside in South Bend, Indiana.